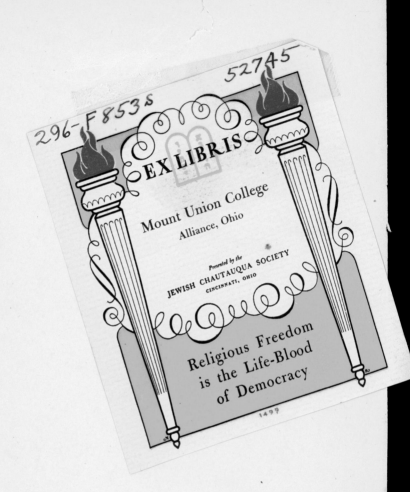

The Small
SANCTUARY

The SMALL SANCTUARY

JUDAISM IN THE PRAYERBOOK

BY

SOLOMON B. FREEHOF, D.D.

THE RIVERDALE PRESS

Cincinnati · 1942

DEDICATED

IN LOVING MEMORY

TO MY MOTHER

GOLDA FREEHOF

*"Her children rise and
call her blessed."*

Editor's Introduction

FOR a number of years Christian students of religion have expressed a desire for a popular work on the Jewish Prayerbook. Some scholarly and detailed studies are available only in German and in Hebrew. Other works, available in English, give an account of the structure of the prayerbook and detailed descriptions of the different types of services, but hitherto we had no work that traced some of the fundamental ideals of Judaism as they are reflected in the prayerbook itself.

This unique approach is followed by Dr. Solomon B. Freehof in the present work entitled *The Small Sanctuary*. Beginning with an analysis of the Jewish experience of worship, the author presents some of the leading Jewish ideals and shows how these are reflected in the content and at times in the very structure of the service. In this way our mood of prayer, our God-idea, our love of Torah, and many other basic Jewish concepts are not only explained and described, but their place in the Prayerbook is also indicated.

The author, Dr. Solomon B. Freehof, gave many years to the study of the Jewish liturgy.

Both as Professor of Liturgy at the Hebrew Union College and as Rabbi of some of the leading congregations in the land, he has made this work his special labor of love.

The book will thus be of interest not only to those who want a popular presentation of the subject, but also to those students who are eager for a more intimate knowledge of the Jewish Prayerbook and the sources of which it is composed which have, to so great an extent, influenced the Christian tradition.

A word should be said to Christian scholars concerning the plan of Hebrew transliteration followed in this book. No scheme of transliteration can satisfy all requirements, as those who have ever tried to prepare one, know only too well. The basic idea underlying our scheme of transliteration is that of making it possible for the individual who does not know Hebrew, to pronounce the word as nearly as possible in accordance with what the sound would be if he read it in Hebrew. We followed the Ashk'nazic pronunciation which is used by the large majority of American Jews. To avoid confusion various Hebrew terms quoted from other sources were modified in accordance with our own plan of transliteration, except where the title of a book was given, in which case, we used the transliteration adopted by the particular author.

We should also note that where the *Union Prayerbook* is mentioned in the book, unless we otherwise indicate, the reference is to the Newly Revised edition of the *Union Prayerbook*, Volume I.

EMANUEL GAMORAN

Acknowledgments

THE AUTHOR acknowledges his great indebtedness to his colleagues, Dr. Samuel H. Goldenson and Dr. Bernard J. Bamberger, for their editorial reading of the manuscript; to Dr. Emanuel Gamoran for his valuable criticisms and suggestions; to Miss Goldie Katz and Mrs. Solomon B. Freehof for their great assistance in the preparation of the manuscript; to Rabbi Philip Frankel, for the preparation of the Index. He is grateful to the publishers listed below for permission to print quotations from their books, as follows:

Jewish Publication Society, Philadelphia.
    Davis, Nina, *Songs of Israel*, 1901. *Jewish Classics Series.*
    Salaman, Nina, *Selected Poems of Jehudah Halevi*, 1924.
    Zangwill, Israel, *Selected Religious Poems of Solomon Ibn Gabirol*, 1923.
George Routledge & Sons, Ltd., London.
    Services of the Synagogue, 1904-1920.
Dodd, Mead & Co., New York.
    Standard Book of Jewish Verse, compiled by Joseph Friedlander, 1917.

S. B. F.

Table of Contents

EDITOR'S INTRODUCTION   vii

ACKNOWLEDGMENTS   xi

I. *I Shall Lift Up Mine Eyes*
THE JEWISH EXPERIENCE OF WORSHIP   3

II. *For All Nations*
THE PRAYERBOOK AND WORLD RELIGION   18

III. *The Small Sanctuary*
THE PRAYERBOOK AND THE SYNAGOGUE   27

IV. *Evening, Morn, and Noon*
THE REGULARITY OF THE SERVICE   36

V. *In the Words of David*
THE PSALMS AND THE STYLE OF THE
PRAYERBOOK   48

VI. *Before Whom Thou Standest*
THE SH'MA AND THE IDEA OF GOD   59

VII. *I Will Arrange My Prayer*
THE T'FILO AND THE IDEA OF PRAYER   72

VIII. *Commune with Your Heart*
TACHANUN AND PRIVATE DEVOTION   88

IX. *Nor Can the Ignorant Be Pious*
   THE SCRIPTURE AND THE IDEAL OF CULTURE   95

X. *At Dawn I Seek Thee*
   EARLY MORNING PRAYERS   112

XI. *Gift of New Soul*
   THE SABBATH SERVICE   122

XII. *Thou Shalt Rejoice*
   THE FESTIVAL SERVICE   144

XIII. *The Book of Life*
   THE HIGH HOLIDAY SERVICE   162

XIV. *I Turn to Thee*
   SPECIAL PRAYERS   178

XV. *I Will Sing unto the Lord*
   HYMNS IN THE PRAYERBOOK   196

XVI. *How Precious Thy Thoughts*
   GEMS FROM THE PRAYERBOOK   217

XVII. *Sing a New Song*
   MEDIEVAL POETRY   237

XVIII. *When Thou Sittest in Thy House*
   HOME PRAYERS   257

XIX. *I Will Praise His Word*
   COMMENTARY ON A SERVICE   269
· xiv ·

xx. *Times and Seasons*

THE CALENDAR   288

BIBLIOGRAPHY   298

INDEX   300

The Small
SANCTUARY

・I・

I Shall Lift Up Mine Eyes

THE JEWISH EXPERIENCE OF WORSHIP

ET not the wise man glory in his wisdom, neither let the mighty man glory in his might, let not the rich man glory in his riches; but let him that glorieth glory in this, that he understandeth, and knoweth Me" (Jer. 9: 22-23).

No real knowledge of God, no true prayer can be found in the heart of a self-satisfied man. He is confident of his own strength. He is proud of his own will. He is sure of his own intellect. He is, therefore, convinced that whatever he may reasonably desire he will be able to achieve by his own efforts. Then why should he pray? He may come to a synagogue or church but his attendance is generally a concession to custom or perhaps an interest in the theme of the sermon to be delivered by the minister. He can rarely be stirred by a desire for devotion. He has too powerful a conviction of his own competence to be able to bow the head and humble the heart. He is so self-satisfied that he can never really pray.

As there are self-satisfied individuals, so there are self-confident periods in human history. In a self-satisfied era the art of prayer is neglected and the very state of mind out of which it might develop disintegrates and disappears. We have just lived through such an epoch of widespread self-sufficiency. The world of the past generation had made many discoveries in many different sciences. It was convinced that whatever man may possibly need will some day be achieved by man's own unaided efforts. All the needs of the body, all the desires of the soul could surely be obtained through mankind's own energy. We lived in a self-satisfied era. Why did we need God? Were we not enough in ourselves? Were we not successful? Our sense of dependence upon a Higher Power grew weak; our houses of worship were neglected and no energetic reorganization, no modernization of religious institutions could make up for the self-confident unprayerfulness of the era. The lines of communication between man and God were neglected and we allowed ourselves to forget the language, the mood, and the spirit of worship.

The average man might never have minded, or might never even have noticed this drastic change in man's spiritual habits had it not been for the fact that the world about us has dramatically and terrifyingly changed. Suddenly our security has become insecurity; our economic world seems to be near disintegration. Great empires are facing destruction. Terror is sweeping through the world. The older mood of self-confidence has evaporated. Man has begun to feel small again. He has begun to acknowledge to himself that with all his sciences, his modern technology, his international business systems, he is still not powerful enough to bring security and happiness to the world.

People have begun to realize also that the most direct threat to world security is a spiritual one. Those who are planning to overthrow our inherited civilization are first attacking our hearts, our brains, and our wills before they attack our shores, our cities, and our factories. We are being subjected to a ceaseless effort to break down our morale. As we face this attack we become aware of the lack of inner stamina to resist. We wonder where we can find again the spiritual strength we need.

Past generations in similar periods of world peril, when man seemed weak in the face of destructive forces, have always sought and often found their strength in a renewed contact with Infinity. They asked the question, "Whence shall come my help?" and answered, "I lift up mine eyes unto the hills." If the spiritual history of the past is any guide to what may occur in the present, we may anticipate a deepening of man's spiritual nature and a new search for communion with the Infinite Strength. Mankind, no longer smug and self-confident, will seek to revive the historic moods and attitudes which helped tide him over tragedies in the past.

A revival of interest in prayer will not at first be spiritual, but intellectual. As the subject re-enters the mind, the average thinking person will recall some of the troublesome problems which prayer always involves. Since this is a questioning and doubting age, the difficulties and problems of prayer will enter the mind of the inquirer more readily than its benefits and its blessings. An answer must be found for questions such as these: what can prayer actually accomplish? Can we expect it to change the rule of nature? How can our words bring health in sickness or strength in weakness? Do we expect to change God's will by our petitions? Why do we need to offer our petitions to God since He is All-Knowing? Is He not aware of our needs before we utter them? Why do prayers praise God so much? Is He gratified by our praises? Do we hope to please Him? Do we mean to win Him with words to change His decrees? Is not prayer hopeless from the beginning since the world is ruled by inexorable law? Is it not useless since the Omniscient already knows our needs? And are not prayers somewhat servile with their constant paeans of praise?

There is, of course, no complete answer to questions such as these, at least no answer that will entirely satisfy everybody. Each person who prays or who thinks about prayer deals with these troublesome questions more or less in his own way. Some fail to find a satisfactory answer for them and thus never learn to pray whole-heartedly. Some find a partial answer which satisfies them. Some grow to feel that the questions are not so important as at first they seemed to be. As is the case with many basic philosophic and spiritual questions, the answer depends considerably on the mood of the questioner and the spirit of the age in which he lives. This new age with its self-confidence broken down and its self-sufficiency melted away, will yet turn toward spiritual matters with more than intellectual curiosity, though this alone would also be valuable. There is in the mood of our times a wistfulness, a desire for inner confidence and spiritual strength. A mood such as this is, in itself, a prelude to a satisfactory working solution of the problems of prayer.

Since the problem of prayer is an old one, we may well find help in dealing with it if we avail ourselves of the long experience of the past. Nowhere in human history has there been a fuller and more creative experience in prayer than in the history of the Jewish people. This ancient community seemed destined from the very beginning to develop the mood and the practice and to create the literature of prayer. Its characteristic group experience broke down those self-complacencies which always made prayer difficult to achieve and created those hungers for which prayer was the natural spiritual food.

The Midrash, commenting on a verse in Exodus (27:20), characterizes Jewish history in a way which helps explain why the people of Israel were the chief discoverers of the art and practice of prayer. The verse in Exodus speaks of the commandment to prepare a light before the Holy of Holies which shall burn continually. The text is as follows, "And thou shalt command the children of Israel that they bring unto thee pure olive oil beaten for the light." The words which impressed the ancient commentators were "pure olive oil beaten"; and their comment upon the phrase points out the fact that the names of many of the plants which grew in Palestine were used metaphorically as descriptive of the people of Israel. Thus, Israel has been described as a fig tree, a palm tree, a vine, etc. But the favorite metaphor of all is the olive tree.

According to the Midrash, the reason that the

olive tree is a favorite biblical symbol of Israel is that the treatment given the olive tree and its fruit corresponds closely to what has happened to the people of Israel. They call attention to the fact that the fruit is plucked from the tree, then it is put upon the ground and beaten, placed in a vat and crushed, and then tied together to be ground up. Thus, the pure olive oil, suitable for sacred purposes, is produced. So it has been with Israel. Crushed and beaten, chained, oppressed and in trouble, it has lifted its voice in prayer to God. Thus, the pure olive oil, the lamp of radiant illumination, the spirit of devotion which burns before the sanctuary, was a product of the sorrows and tragedies which crushed the spirit of Israel. The implication of this ancient analogy is clear. Had our people lived a life of unbroken political power, of dominant military might, and of endless prosperity, it would have been too self-satisfied to have lifted up its voice so sincerely to the source of all strength. Its very tragedy, the constant bruising of its soul produced the radiant eternal light of prayer and communion with God.

Of course, grief and misfortune alone would not be enough to have inspired a great devotional literature. Such misfortunes might very well have broken the spirit of the people and left them hopeless and mute. But it so happened that the great sorrows of defeat, poverty, and exile, came to them after they already possessed a deep, spiritual experience embodied in a noble religious literature. A people which was spiritually blessed with a great literature and also delivered from self-satisfaction and self-conceit by an endless succession of misfortunes was well equipped to become a pioneer in prayer.

If the ancient Greeks, like the Hebrews, had been deeply interested in prayer, they would have bequeathed to posterity a brilliant theoretical analysis of its philosophy. But Israel has left us the Synagogue and the Prayerbook. The Israelites were not particularly concerned as were the Greeks with the theoretical implications of an idea, but with its practical application to human life. The Greeks might ask, "What is the nature of God?" The Jew asks, "What doth the Lord require of me?" Hence, to find the Jewish concept of God the chief source would not be the works of the philosophers, but the Bible itself in which God Himself is represented as the Hero of history. If we wish to know the philosophy of Jewish law we do not look in a book on the theory of Jewish jurisprudence, but we consult the practical laws and maxims of the Bible and the Talmud. Similarly, to study the Jewish doctrine of prayer and its practice, our best source is not some theoretical work on the subject but partly in the history of the Synagogue as an institution and chiefly in the historic Jewish Prayerbook itself. As we restudy the actual prayer texts used by our people for many centuries, we shall find implied in them the philosophy and doctrine and the mood of Jewish worship. This is perhaps the primary purpose of this book, namely, to find in the Prayerbook the Jewish ideal of worship.

Through Christianity and Mohammedanism the Jewish concepts and methods of prayer have influenced the religion of the world. Since Jewish prayer finds its fullest expression in the Prayerbook, the book must be looked upon as one of the classics of man's spiritual history. That is to say, that the Jewish Prayerbook must be given a much higher evaluation than it has generally been accorded. Hitherto, the Bible was usually regarded as the sole vehicle of Jewish spiritual influence in the world. This judgment is not correct.

Judaism emerged from classical times with three great literary monuments: the Bible, the Prayerbook, and the Talmud. The Talmud has had no direct effect upon the life of the non-Jewish world. Being the record of the discussions, interpretations, and traditions, which built up the legal system governing Jewish life, its effect was almost entirely restricted to the life of the Jewish community. Of course, insofar as the Jewish community itself constituted a spiritual and intellectual leaven all over the world, to that extent the Talmud, which helped preserve the unique Jewish people, may be deemed likewise to have exerted an influence on the larger world. But, of course, such influence was indirect; besides, the Talmud was only one of many instrumentalities which helped preserve the Jewish community.

The third great literary work brought by Jewry out of antiquity, namely, the Prayerbook, had a direct influence upon the development of human history. But while the influence of the Bible is openly acknowledged, that of the Jewish Prayerbook is not generally known. The very existence of a special prayer-literature in the form of a Prayerbook intended for use by the average man was a new development in the history of religion. There were ancient collections of hymns among the Babylonians. These were used by the priests as an accessory to the sacrificial cult. But a Prayerbook to be used by every man, priest or layman, specifically for the purpose of spiritual expression, had never appeared hitherto. Its very existence evidenced a great increase in the spirit of devotion which through Christianity, and later through Mohammedanism, gave a new inwardness to the religion of a large proportion of mankind. The Jews were the world's chief teachers of the art and habit of prayer.

The concept of prayer inherent in the Prayerbook has played an incalculable part in the development of Christianity and Mohammedanism. Moreover, the Synagogue, the institution for which the Prayerbook was developed, had so thoroughgoing an influence on Christian ritual and Christian religious organization that it may well be said that Christianity might not have outlasted the disintegration of the Roman Empire had it not been guided by the Jewish mode of worship. Thus, quite directly, the Jewish Prayerbook, like the Jewish Bible, played a highly significant part in the creation of the modern world.

However, the first direct influence of the Prayerbook was on the development of Jewish life. In this regard the Prayerbook must be understood in its relationship to the other great works produced by the Jewish past. In a time sequence the Prayerbook may be looked upon as a link between Bible and Talmud, each link in the chain overlapping the preceding one. Thus, the Prayerbook arose before the later books of the Bible were completed and the early days of talmudic development exercised a considerable influence on the Prayerbook which had achieved its classic form while the Talmud was still in its earlier stages.

The literary and spiritual tradition which these three books represent never completely came to an end. Long after the Bible canon was closed and no more books admitted into Sacred Scripture, biblical study continued and has become a permanent part of world literature. Long after the Talmud was finished (about the year five hundred), talmudic studies continued through the ages. But even with regard to this continuance of creative work, the Prayerbook differs from the other two books. While the Bible itself was finally completed about the middle of the second century of the present era and the Talmud in the sixth century, the Prayerbook itself was never actually completed. All through the centuries new prayers in prose and poetry were added to it. In the periods when mystic moods dominated Jewish life, mystic and cabalistic prayers were added to the Prayerbook. In periods when philosophic studies flourished, philosophic ideas were inserted, and during times of persecution and exile, poems of tragedy were added.

These various additions were used by the congregations as authentic parts of the Prayerbook. Indeed, when the Reform movement began no one dreamed of making additions or changes in the Bible or the Talmud. These books were finished and complete for all time. But it was natural to make changes, additions, and subtractions in the Prayerbook since it was expected to fit the mood and the ideas of the people. Thus, of the three works which Judaism brought out of antiquity, the Prayerbook was the only one which constantly changed to fit the needs and the moods and the aspirations of the people of Israel.

Perhaps another distinction must be made between the Prayerbook and the other two books. While it was a duty incumbent upon every Jew to read the Scriptures regularly, particularly the weekly portions from the Law and the Prophets, and while it was incumbent upon all to study the Law as embodied in the Talmud, there were many who did not find it possible to study the difficult talmudic argumentation or even to read regularly the classic text of Scripture. But every Jew used the Prayerbook three times a day. Its text exerted a direct, daily influence on the life of every Jew.

Because the Prayerbook always changed to fit the changing moods and because it was read daily and thus directly influenced the life of every Jew, it has become a valuable source for the study of Judaism as a living faith. It can provide certain insights which we might not find even in the Bible or the Talmud. The Bible contains the highest ideals of Judaism as they revealed themselves to the great religious geniuses, Moses, Isaiah, Jeremiah, the Psalmists. The Talmud represented the details of religious conduct, legal and ethical, as analyzed by the keen intellects of the talmudic teachers. But the Prayerbook contained those religious ideals from biblical, talmudic, and other sources, which were actually a part of the life of every man in Israel. Therefore, not merely what Judaism should at its best strive to be, nor what keen logical analysis may reason out as its obligatory duty, but what Judaism actually was in the life of the average man can be seen, more than in any other literary source, in the Jewish Prayerbook.

The purpose of this book will be to give a general picture of Jewish religious ideas and ideals as they reveal themselves in the Prayerbook. Since it is intended not for the technical scholar but for the average reader, it will not attempt to achieve an exhaustive catalogue and organization of all ideas, philosophic, cabalistic, folkloristic, which may be found in the Prayerbook. It will, rather, give the general outline of the religious mood as it reflected itself in everyday Jewish life through the Prayerbook. It will describe the great historic ideas and moods expressed in the Prayerbook text and in its very structure, and will attempt to indicate to some extent how these ideas were modified by changing influences of the passing ages.

Toward the end of his career Moses reminded the people of Israel that during their forty years of wandering in the wilderness, their garments had not decayed (Deut. 8:4). To explain this miracle the Midrash (Cant. R. to Cant. 4:11) says, "Clouds of glory swept down from heaven and brushed against the garments of our ancestors and kept them sweet and clean." Thus it was possible for these garments, as the Midrash implies, to grow with the growth of the child and retain their beauty and their usefulness all through life. The sincere striving for God's presence as expressed through the aspirations of prayer were "clouds of glory" which during the years of Israel's wandering through the desert of history, kept the Prayerbook sweet and clean, a living and growing garment of the living soul of Israel.

II

For All Nations

THE PRAYERBOOK AND WORLD RELIGION

THE statement in Ecclesiastes that "there is
nothing new under the sun" is undoubt-
edly true, and it applies even to that statement itself. Some older sage living centuries before the biblical author must have realized and
expressed the same truth. As even the newest
house is built of stones which are millions of years
old, or of concrete, or iron made out of elements
which are as old as the earth itself, so in the realm
of ideas every thought has some kinship with
previous thought, every philosophy is related to
some earlier philosophy, every belief to some
earlier belief. There is an unbroken thread of
continuity in human ideas reaching back into the
unrecorded past.

When we speak of the great ethical and religious discoveries of Judaism we must understand, of course, that these have considerable
connection with earlier ideas out of which they
grew. The biblical doctrines are more beautiful

and noble than the sources from which they sprung, but they still are closely connected with them. Out of the material of ancient religious notions and attitudes, Judaism built a new structure, a magnificent new mansion for the human spirit.

Monotheism, the conviction that there is one universal mind, one Master of the world, existed in embryo in many ancient religions and was even explicit for one brief moment in ancient Egyptian history. It was found at the highest reaches of the thought of certain great philosophers. But Judaism took the idea of monotheism, cleansed it of all impurity, and spread it among the people. Thus, the monotheistic idea became not only the exceptional and daring insight of a few exalted individuals, but also the living conviction of an entire nation. Monotheism was made independent of the fate of a few exceptional individuals and became an indestructible and permanent influence on the religion and even the science of the world.

The concept that the one God is so spiritual and pure as to be indescribable by any image made by man, must have been realized by certain sages and isolated thinkers in many places and at many times. Yet these lofty thoughts disappeared when the thinkers died. The good was "interred with their bones." But the prophets of

Israel were never content with merely thinking of God's pure spirituality. They waged a war of the spirit against images and statues which misled men and coarsened their concept of God. Beginning with Moses they conducted a ceaseless battle against all idolatry. These pioneers wanted to create an entire *nation* of philosophers, a people in which the humblest man should learn to realize God as pure spirit. Thus they fought and struggled and wrestled with their people, forbidding them the joy of the plastic arts at least in relation to depicting God, mocking their human weaknesses, hectoring them without respite until they became the first people on earth to learn to visualize God, the Great One, without the aid of delimiting images. Israel was the first entire people to think of God as pure Spirit; thus, it helped permanently to purify the religion of all men.

The idea of ethical responsibility is as old as man. As far back as we can go in the human story we find not only "I want" but "I ought." Yet this ethical responsibility was always narrow, incumbent only upon members of the tribe or the clan in relation to one another. The old *mores* and *ethoi*, as the very words imply, mean the customary mutual obligations of the restricted group. But limited as it was, it was nevertheless the ethical impulse, precious and waiting like a seed to be planted in fertile soil. Judaism took the seed of tribal ethics and brought it to its greatest fruition. It connected the ethical impulse with the universal spiritual God. It visualized Him as just, merciful, and holy. It gave men the ideal of rising above the limits of their habitual group comradeship, their old tribal decencies, and bade them strive to imitate an Infinite Nobility. "Holy shall ye be, for I the Lord your God am holy." By making monotheism ethical it made morality dynamic and universal.

These great religious and ethical influences were exercised by Judaism over the world through the Bible. But through the Prayerbook, also, it exercised an influence perhaps equally important. Whereas, through the Bible Judaism taught the world an ideal of religion nobler than any known before, through the Prayerbook and the Synagogue, it taught the world a mode of communion with God which made this noble religion liveable, intimate, and effective in daily life. The Bible is the meaning of Judaism; the Prayerbook, its method. The Bible is doctrine. The Prayerbook is spiritual training.

Of course, as is the case with every other great religious achievement in Judaism, the roots of the Prayerbook go deep into the past. The impulse toward prayer is as old as religion itself. The primitive savages wove spells to control their gods. They uttered magic words. They shouted commands at natural objects to drive them to obey the will of man. In later epochs man developed elaborate sacrificial rituals and occasionally accompanied them with hymns or prayers. The old Babylonian rituals taken from ancient Sumerian times were repeated for centuries in a language unknown to the worshipers. There is also record of occasional noble personal prayers addressed to the deity by classic philosophers. Certain exalted hymns were at one period addressed to Egyptian gods. All these various prayer elements had long existed in the world. In Judaism, too, there were ancient customs of occasional prayer and even old prayer phrases dating back to the patriarchs and the early kings. There is specific provision for certain prayers to be recited in connection with the Temple ritual as, for example, the prayer text to be recited on bringing the first ripe fruits to the Temple (Deut. 26:1-11). We are given the text of the ancient blessing which the priests recited over the children of Israel (Num. 6:22-27). An ancient tradition (m. Yomo vi, 2) tells us that when the priest pronounced the holy name of God the people assembled uttered the prayer, "Praised be His glorious name forever and ever." In fact, informal, personal prayers must have accompanied many of the sacrifices, particularly the Tomid, the regular daily sacrifices. The Mishnah (m. Tomid vii, 3) tells that during the song of the Levites which followed the morning sacrifices in the Temple, the people prostrated themselves. Ben Sirach, describing the Temple service, speaks of this prostration by the people present in the Temple courts during the sacrifice and adds (Ecclesiasticus 50:19): "And the people besought the Lord the most high by prayer before Him that is merciful." It was natural that the people should pray for their own desires and needs while the priests offered the sacrifices. Out of all this heritage of prayer Judaism made something new, unprecedented, and revolutionary in its influence.

The prayer-service recorded in the Prayerbook represents something fundamentally different from the various broken fragments of primitive religion. Instead of an occasional prayer or hymn appended to the more important sacrificial ritual, this was a complete spiritual service by itself and for itself. Instead of a ritual conducted by a special priest group, this was a service to be recited by every human being. Instead of those occasional outbursts of prayer, found even among primitive men in time of famine or military defeat or fear of invasion, this service was regular, three times a day, in every season and in every stage of life. The Jewish

Prayerbook represented what had hitherto never before existed on earth, a regular, democratic, purely spiritual worship of God, with no ritual deemed more essential than the utterance of the aspiring soul.

The influence of this prayer-service, regular, democratic, and purely spiritual, upon the religion and, therefore, upon the history of man, is beyond calculation; but a few illustrations will indicate how far-reaching its influence was.

It seems evident, for example, that without this mode of worship the Christian church might never have survived the early days of persecution in the Roman Empire. While many an oriental religion was encouraged by the Roman emperors and even subsidized and provided with magnificent temples in the Imperial City itself, the Christian church, together with Judaism, the parent faith, knew nothing but persecution. Then what kept Christianity alive? It was not merely that the Christian church taught noble doctrines. Many of the mystery-religions had ennobling doctrines of salvation, and the religion of Mithra had a high ideal of life and an inspiring influence upon its devotees. It is not unlikely that the real power of Christianity to survive those early persecutions was based upon the mode of worship which it learned in Palestine. Had it been dependent for its worship upon a sacrificial ritual conducted in one particular sacred spot with solemn ceremony and by special priests as all other religions were, then having been driven from Rome, constantly persecuted and scattered, denied any recognition as a religion, it could easily have been submerged. But Christianity had learned the lesson of prayer-worship in Israel. In the earliest years the Christians, being Jews, continued to attend the synagogue. They learned that wherever people gathered, whoever they were, priest or layman, they could worship God with sincere words which came from the heart. "Wherever My Name is mentioned, I will come to thee and bless thee." Driven into the catacombs and the forests, they established there their little synagogues and conducted their regular spiritual worship as the Jews did. Thus the church was ubiquitous and indestructible. It was because the church was really a synagogue and its worship prayer-worship that it lived to come in from the forests and up from the catacombs and set its bishops upon the throne of the Caesars.

The same influence is felt in a later religion, also the offspring of Judaism, the religion of Mohammed. True it has its sacred temple in Mecca to which all Mohammedans must come as pilgrims once in their lifetime, but it has mosques which are synagogues scattered all over the world and its worship is a prayer-worship. Therefore, wherever the faithful are, in the mountains of Afghanistan, on the windy plateaus of Persia, on the burning sands of the Sahara, they can gather and lift their hearts in prayer to God and know that these prayers are acceptable to Him as worship. Because of the worship of God through regular prayer, taught first in Israel, two great religions have lived and spread over the world and changed the course of history. With no other mode of worship but a regular prayer-worship could either of these faiths have become a world religion.

III

The Small Sanctuary

THE PRAYERBOOK AND THE SYNAGOGUE

THE Prayerbook did not develop as an isolated phenomenon. The regular prayer-worship, recorded in the Prayerbook and conducted in the synagogue, was so different from the devotional fragments found in other faiths that it constitutes literally a religious revolution, and could have come into existence only as part of a general mood of spiritual creativity. Such a new mood arose during the Babylonian Exile and in the post-Exilic period. A combination of exceptional achievements appeared at this age in Jewish history, and all of them combined to create this particular religious climax.

The phenomenon of the Exile itself was an unusual one. Hundreds of nations had been exiled in the recurrent sweep and counter-sweep of conquering imperial armies in ancient times. But of all the peoples who were dislocated from their national homes this one people managed to return from its exile and reestablish its state. The tragic exile, which must have seemed at the time to be the end of an epoch, became merely one of the distant experiences in a far-off half-forgotten past. Why did Israel survive the Exile? The chief reason for Israel's survival through that seemingly final tragedy was the influence of the prophets of Israel. They instilled in the hearts of the people the concept of the universal God whose glory filled all the earth. Other peoples believed that their god was the particular god of their country; therefore, when the people was defeated the god himself was thought to be defeated by a more powerful god and his image was dragged away into exile to be a slave in the temple of the conquering god. The people of Israel could not fall into the belief that their God was defeated, for the very fact of the Exile was a fulfilment of His word predicted by His prophets. God was not an exile in Babylon. He was a King "and the whole world was filled with His glory." The people exiled from Palestine were, therefore, not exiled from the presence of their God as other people would have believed themselves to be. They could never escape from His presence even if they took up "the wings of the morning and flew to the uttermost parts of the earth." Furthermore, the prophets had long denounced the insincerity of much of the ceremonialism of the older Temple worship and taught that God should be worshipped in righteousness. Thus, they created the assurance in the hearts of the people that even with the loss of the Temple those who "made their hearts clean and put away the evil of their doings" could come into the presence of God. Therefore, although at first "by the waters of Babylon we sat down and wept," for "how shall we sing the Lord's song in a foreign land," they soon recollected the teachings of the prophets that God was everywhere and could be worshipped by the sincere soul. They gathered in the cities and villages of Babylon to maintain their community spirit and their communion with God. Thus Judaism survived what might well have been its death blow. The informal gatherings of the people in the Exile proved to be the beginnings of the synagogue and its spiritual worship which became part of their religious practice when they returned to establish their state in the Holy Land for another era of creative life.

The period of the Return from the Exile was a time of extraordinary creative achievement. It is strange that it should have been so. The community was a tiny one at first, living among the ruins of former grandeur. Very little happened to it to be recorded in history. There are great stretches of time in the four and a half centuries of the Second Commonwealth about which we have no record at all. Yet in this period, sparse at first in outward events, the inner life of Israel seemed to awake to a new flowering and almost every achievement helped to build the habit of spiritual worship.

The most famous name among those who returned from the Exile was Ezra, whose title "The Scribe" indicates clearly his intellectual aspirations and those of his fellows. Scholars agree that Ezra and his circle initiated a period of eager literary activity. He and his followers gathered documents, organized texts, built up a great deal of what came to be regarded as Sacred Scripture. They studied the Scriptures and developed some of the legal implications of the ancient laws. Thus, the period of the Second Commonwealth began with literary activity, but the development of this literary interest went far beyond the creation of literature.

Sacred literature is found in many ancient cultures but these holy scriptures were studied only by learned priests. The average person could neither read nor write nor were the contents of the sacred books meant to be the concern of the average worshiper. The masses were taught to see their religion as pageantry, ritual, music, and drama. Only the chosen few read and studied and knew the content of the holy books of the ancient faiths.

Therefore, the mere fact that Ezra and his scribes helped develop Sacred Scripture was, in itself, nothing exceptional in the history of religion. They were a priestly group, literate and learned. What became of the Scriptures and how they came to be used in worship was exceptional and unprecedented. The people who had grown accustomed during the Exile to listen to the words of their exiled prophets and perhaps to hear the reading of the writings of earlier prophets, once despised and now respected, evidently desired, now that they had returned, to continue such instruction and edification. Thus they again assembled to listen to the word of God. These assemblies were at first occasional and irregular but they were a beginning. At these occasional meetings not only were the works of the prophets read to the people but soon the Five Books of Moses, the Law, Israel's legal constitution, were also read to them. Soon it became a regular custom to read and expound the Law and the Prophets in these various assemblages. Thus for the first time in human history the sacred books of a faith ceased to be secret books. Learning was no longer confined to the professional priestly élite. All the people were taught to listen, to understand, to discuss, and to reason. The reading of the Scriptures in the scattered popular meeting-places was the first evidence of democratic education in the story of man's mental growth. When these meeting-places developed into the synagogue, the reading and the study of Sacred Scripture became a fixed part of the ritual and the ceremonies involved in taking out the Scroll and returning it to the Ark, the blessings, and the prayers before and after the reading, were a permanent part of the Jewish Prayerbook.

In this creative epoch another development took place as surprising as the first attempt at democratic education through the popular reading and study of Scripture. From pre-Exilic times among the Sacred Scrolls preserved there were not only codes of law in the name of Moses, the great teacher who led Israel out of Egypt, not only great orations associated with the names of unforgettable prophets, but also poems of various types, some ancient ones of the warlike epic type, songs of battle and victory, and others tender, simple, and spiritual, true lyric poetry, the outpourings of the heart.

Many of these spiritual poems associated with the name of David were remembered and sung and, few as they may have been, they constituted a treasured part of the literary heritage carried over from pre-Exilic times. For lyric poetry generally represents the climax of a literary evolution. In the early days of a civilization man is hardly aware of his separate personality, of his own desires and sorrows. He thinks and speaks and lives and dies as a member of a tribe. His earliest literature is tribal literature, and his earliest poetry is tribal epic poetry. It is only when civilization advances far that the individual personality becomes aware of itself and the lyric poetry of self-awareness eventually appears. That such lyric poems should have been created in ancient pre-Exilic times was perhaps an evidence of spiritual precocity and that such lyric writing increased after the return from Babylon indicated the attainment of full literary maturity. Perhaps the bulk of the Psalms were written in those generations. The Psalms, most of them anonymous, written by humble people expressing their fears and their hopes and their woes and their triumphs, constitute one of the greatest collections of personal lyric poetry bequeathed to us by antiquity. These Psalms, perhaps at first sung individually by their authors, then repeated by the townsmen, then taken to express the sorrows of the entire people, found their way into the little assemblies gathered for the study of Scripture, became permanently a part of Jewish worship, and entered and remained forever in the Jewish Prayerbook.

Ezra and his scribes were priests. It was the traditional function of the priest to be the guardian of the Law. "For the priest's lips should keep knowledge and they should seek the law at his mouth" (Mal. 2:7). But the very fact that the priestly function of law-making should have expanded into a widespread study of the Law by the entire people as they listened to the reading and interpretation of Scripture in the synagogues, indicates a tide in this epoch in the direction of democracy. This democratic impulse gradually grew stronger through the influence of the Pharisaic movement which dominated the later part of the epoch. The Pharisees, much maligned in the New Testament, represented the people's party, the rights of the individual Israelite against the prerogatives of the hereditary priesthood. It was their ideal to make Judaism the practice of every man until every home became a temple and every father a priest. All the home ceremonies, the Kiddush, the blessings over food, etc., are traceable to the democratizing Pharisaic influence. Naturally, it was the Pharisees who emphasized the importance of the little popular assemblies, the synagogues, and strengthened them as a counterpoise to the Temple at Jerusalem which was dominated by the hereditary priesthood.

Thus we see that the Synagogue and its

Prayerbook came into being from a merger of many influences which appeared during the Second Commonwealth. Each one of these separate influences was unusual and each had its unique gift to bring to Israel's new method of the worship of God. From the reading and study of Scripture, the world's first democratic education, the synagogue became forever a house of study. From the lyrical influence of the psalm poetry, the synagogue became forever a house of prayer and devotion. From the Pharisaic democratic movement, the synagogue became forever a house of assembly of the people. The omission of any one of these influences would have left the synagogue incomplete. All three of them together made synagogue-prayer what it was, the world's first democratic, purely spiritual worship of God.

IV

Evening, Morn, and Noon

THE REGULARITY OF THE SERVICE

WHEN the exiles returned from Babylon, one of their first tasks was the
rebuilding of the Temple on Mount
Zion so that they could offer the regular sacrifices and the special offerings of thanks and
atonement ordained by Mosaic Law. This Temple was the center of worship. It was the direct
successor of the tabernacle built in those far-off
days of the Exodus from Egypt. Within its pre-
cincts were conducted the prescribed sacrifices
ordained by Holy Writ. These ancient rituals
were maintained with scrupulous care by the
aristocratic descendants of the honored family
of Aaron.

In contrast to the high status and dignity of
the Temple, the small synagogues which gradually appeared over the land for the study of
Scripture, the recital of psalms and prayers,
seemed unimportant. These little meeting-places
had no scriptural warrant. They had no pre-

scribed ritual and no ancient priestly aristocracy to maintain and nurture them.

Yet for the reasons mentioned in the preceding chapter, the little meeting-houses grew in importance. The average man was developing a sense of his own spiritual significance. His impulse toward religious self-expression was being fostered by the democratic movements in Israel. But the popular assemblies, the synagogues, were still lacking in dignity and status compared with the central Temple governed by the aristocratic priesthood. The people's houses of prayer would never come into their own as long as their assemblies or services were merely occasional. If the synagogue could only develop a regularly ordained holiday and week-day service, as the Temple possessed, such an unbroken regularity of worship would indicate the significance of the synagogue as a sacred house of worship and would stamp the prayers as an adequate mode of worship. But there was no precedent for such uninterrupted succession of prayer-services. There was as yet no religion which maintained a regularity of prayer-worship. Whatever regularity existed in any religion was the regularity of the sacrificial ritual, not of prayer. Offerings were made to the gods, at dawn or at dusk, at certain seasons of the year, but prayers were either an insignificant appendage to the regular sacrificial ritual or were occasional outbursts of supplication at times of special crisis. It never dawned upon the leaders of the other religions of antiquity that prayer in itself, the worshipping of God through the outpouring of the emotions, could ever be of such importance that it should be given the dignity of a regular ritual. Yet as long as such prayer meetings remained occasional and spasmodic, they could never be a permanent influence on the life of the people.

Eventually in the Second Commonwealth the humble synagogues throughout the land attained the status of honored regularity for their prayer and study services. These regular services grew to be quite as respected as were the biblical ordained sacrifices in the Temple itself. This was a great step forward in the history of religion. Never before did any prayer-worship attain such status and such an opportunity for continuous influence upon the life of a community. How did the prayer-worship in the synagogue obtain the dignity and importance of a regular service?

In later years, during the time of the earlier talmudic literature, the regular daily worship had become so firmly fixed as a part of Jewish life that the rabbis felt that it must have been so from time immemorial. In fact, they say that the men of the Great Synagogue (i.e., the successors of Ezra) established for Israel the blessings and the prayers. They even said that the three patriarchs themselves established the three daily services (b. B'rochos 26b). Of course, part of the prayer-worship was quite ancient. The people gathered fairly often for special services, particularly for fast-day services. These fast-day services, with their penitential ritual without any sacrificial accompaniment, may well have taken place even before the Exile. After the Return, the people gathered every Sabbath to listen to the reading from Scripture. But it is evident that the regular daily service could not have taken place except after considerable evolution.

The influence which eventually created the regularity of the daily prayer-service was the ritual of the Temple itself which was, of course, daily and regular. In later years, when the synagogue prayer-service had acquired uninterrupted regularity, the rabbis connected this regularity of prayer with the earlier regularity of sacrifices in the Temple. This is evident from the very term which they used to describe the prayer-worship. They called it Avodo She-ba-lev, "the ritual of the heart" (b. Taanis 2a). The sacrificial Temple ritual was called *Avodo*, which means service (i.e., sacrificial liturgy); and the prayer-worship was, therefore, characterized as "the sacrificial ritual offered in the heart." Furthermore, they stated as a definite principle (b. B'rochos 26b; j. B'rochos IV, 1) that the prayers or, specifically, the petitional prayers, the T'filo, were ordained so as to correspond to the regular daily offerings in the Temple.

How could the humble synagogues dare to copy the august ritual of the ancient Temple? How could these lay institutions assume for their prayers and assemblies the biblically ordained regularity of the priestly ritual? This transfer of dignity could not have occurred as an isolated phenomenon. It was part of a larger democratic tendency which culminated in the Pharisaic movement (discussed in Chapter III). This democratic movement influenced all of Jewish life and penetrated even into the life and conduct of the aristocratic priesthood. While the hereditary priesthood continued to conduct the traditional sacrificial ritual, they themselves gradually came under the influence and control of the Pharisaic movement. An indication of this increasing democratic control over the Temple is the fact that the regular offering for which the priests insisted upon paying with their own funds was, after a time, required to be paid from the public treasury, thus proving that the regular offering was not the offering exclusively of the priests but the people's sacrifice to God

(b. M'nochos, 65a). The Pharisees, likewise, strengthened the older democratic institution of *Ma-a-modos* (Standing Committees). They explained the justification for these committees by asking, "How can a man's sacrifice be offered unless the man is present when the sacrifice is being made?" (m. Taanis IV, 2). Therefore, since the sacrifice came from the entire people and not from the priests alone, a plan was evolved whereby the people or their representatives stood by the priests at every daily sacrifice. The plan was worked out as follows: just as the priestly clan was divided into twenty-four groups (watches), so was Palestine and the people of Israel divided into twenty-four districts with twenty-four committees (*Ma-a-modos*). As each priestly watch came up to Jerusalem to officiate at the Temple for its scheduled week, so each committee of priests, Levites, and Israelites, came up in turn from its district "to stand by" the sacrifices for a week. During the week the people of that district at home gathered at the time of the regular sacrifice to hold services in the local synagogues at the same hour. Thus, there was one week (twice a year) in which the regularity of the Temple's sacrifice itself was translated into the regularity of prayer-service in the home district. From this week of daily service, which took place at the hour of the daily sacrifices in Jerusalem, the daily services spread throughout the year. Thus, at first, there were daily services all year in different districts. Soon there were daily services all year all over the land.

However, this correspondence between the time of the regular sacrifice and the time of services in the synagogue cannot be the entire explanation for the number of prayer-services during the day. It explains the fact that there were regular daily services but the parallel between the time of the offerings in the Temple and the time of the services is not complete. The traditional periods of daily prayer in the synagogue were three: morning (shacharis), afternoon (mincho), and evening (ma-ariv). These three services are quite ancient. The later author of the Book of Daniel visualizes this thrice-daily prayer (at least as private prayer) as having occurred even as far back as the Exile itself. This Book tells us that Daniel would pray three times daily, morning, noon, and night. "His windows were open in his upper chamber towards Jerusalem and he kneeled upon his knees three times a day, and prayed, and gave thanks before his God, as he did aforetimes" (Daniel 6:11). The Psalmist (Psalm 55:18) also speaks of three regular times for prayer. "Evening, and morning and at noonday, will I complain, and moan; and He hath heard my voice."

This custom of regular prayer three times daily could not have arisen entirely in correspondence with the sacrificial service in the Temple on Mount Zion. In the first place, there was no evening prayer in the Temple. At sunset the gates of the Temple were closed and nothing occurred at night except that the priestly and Levite sentinels kept guard and the eternal fire on the great altar burned continually. The fixed times for the Temple ritual were the morning and afternoon regular sacrifice (the Tomid). On the Sabbath and holidays there was the additional sacrifice after the Morning Service (Musof). The committee of laymen during its week at the Temple prayed four times daily, corresponding to these three sacrifices and the fourth service, N'ilo, the closing of the Temple gates at sunset. It is clear that these four periods of prayer by the "committees" in the Temple do not harmonize with the three periods of prayer, morning, afternoon, and evening, which became traditional in the synagogue.

This difficulty engaged the attention of the rabbis and they debated at considerable length. It is not surprising that they have an alternative theory to the one that the prayers correspond to the time of the regular sacrifices, namely, that the prayers were ordained for the three positions of the sun during the day, sunrise, noon, and sunset (j. B'rochos IV, 1). It seems, therefore, that the three periods of synagogue prayers daily are the result of two influences, the influence of the Temple ritual in Jerusalem and the natural impulse to pray at the crucial times of the day, sunrise, noon, and sunset. People who revered God as the Master of nature would surely worship Him at the two crucial times of the day, when the sun rose and when the sun set. At these two times they became accustomed to recite the great prayer taken from Deuteronomy, "Hear O Israel . . . and thou shalt speak of them when thou risest up and when thou liest down." That morning and night are appropriate times for prayers to the Lord of the Universe is indicated also in Psalm 92:2: "It is a good thing to give thanks unto the Lord, and to sing praises unto Thy Name, O Most High, to declare Thy lovingkindness in the morning and Thy faithfulness in the night seasons." The night prayer and the morning prayer, particularly the former, were home prayers recited at the actual time of rising in the morning and retiring at night. But gradually they became synagogue prayers. The morning prayer became merged with the prayer at the time of the morning sacrifice at the Temple. The night prayer at sunset or after sunset had no Temple connection. In addition to these two, the prayer corresponding to the afternoon sacrifice was added, thus making three prayers a day. Besides these three daily services, there is an additional service (musof) held on holidays and new moons. This is derived from the additional holiday and new moon sacrifice (musof) in the Temple. A "gate-closing" prayer (N'ilo) at sunset is still found in the synagogue ritual, not daily, but on the Day of Atonement. Thus, the idea of regular prayer was borrowed from the regular sacrifices in the Temple, but the hour of prayer, three times a day, came partially from the Temple and partially from the natural impulse to worship God at sunrise and sunset.

Our discussion so far has dealt entirely with the historical background of the Prayerbook and of the Synagogue in which it developed. In the following chapters we will deal with the structure and the contents of the book and the moods and philosophy of Judaism which they imply. But already from the study of the historical background itself, one definite characteristic of Judaism has become clear. In the period of the Second Commonwealth during which the Prayerbook developed there were many movements, many impulses, many varied tendencies. That period lasted almost five centuries. They were five centuries of vast change in world history. The era marked the end of the Babylonian domination, the beginning of the Persian Empire and also its decay. It included the revolutionary career of Alexander the Great and the hellenizing of the Mediterranean world and much of Asia. It included the collapse of the Grecian states and the rise of Rome. In such a period of great change Israel's life inevitably underwent constant transformation. New circumstances necessitated new organization. Many institutions died and were born. New ideas grew up, flourished, and decayed. Many parties rose in Israel and disappeared. Many types of literature and many languages were written. Some became permanent; many were lost. In all these changeful times the Prayerbook gathered to itself different ideas but all these various ideas had one mood in common, which through the Prayerbook and the Synagogue became a permanent mood in Judaism. The idea of widespread study of the Law which contributed to the prayer-service, the reading and the interpretation and the discussion of Scripture, the mood of the lyrical psalms which made the prayer-service mystical and poetic, the regularity of the services brought into the synagogue prayers by the growing popular control over the aristocratic priesthood in the Temple in Jerusalem; all these varied impulses and ideas pointed toward one goal, the spirit of democracy in religion.

No longer was the Law and its study the property of priestly scribes and law-givers. It became the duty of all men to read the Law, to meditate upon it, and to understand it. No longer was religious poetry the traditional chant of guilds of professional Levitical singers accompanying the Temple ritual. Now the sorrows and griefs of the humble and the anonymous found expression in religious poetry. No longer was the regular ritual of service to God the solemn observance of hereditary priests, but "the service of the heart" of the humblest Israelite. The very existence of the scattered synagogues testified to the fact that the people of Israel had learned to fulfil the biblical verse seriously: to become a kingdom of priests and a holy people. Every one of them in his actions, in his devotions, and in his "priestly" function was a servant and a child of the living God. These democratic moods, developed in various ways during the Second Commonwealth, never vanished from Judaism. They were united and merged in the prayer-service and became a permanent part of Jewish thinking and feeling. Through the Synagogue which maintained the dignity of the average man, democracy lived in Israel and manifested itself in new impulses, new literature, new movements, throughout the ages to our day. Judaism would never again be a priest-ridden, formal faith.

V

In the Words of David

THE PSALMS AND THE STYLE OF THE PRAYERBOOK

A STUDENT reading the Jewish Prayerbook for the first time would in all likelihood be surprised at the large numbers of biblical psalms embodied in the various services. In the traditional Prayerbook after the early morning blessings, which are really semi-private, the public part of the Morning Service begins with a group of eight psalms. On the Sabbath this group of psalms is augmented by the addition of nine other psalms, and the close of the Morning Service is marked by the reciting of a psalm for each day of the week, one for Monday, one for Tuesday, etc. In the Reform Prayerbook this mass of psalms opening the service is to be noticed particularly in the Service for the Day of Atonement while all other services open with a psalm sung by the choir and contain whole psalms and psalm verses throughout the service. A count of words in the Prayerbook would show that virtually half of the bulk of the main prayers is composed of quotations, whole chapters, or single verses of the Book of Psalms. The Psalms constitute the greatest biblical influence on the Prayerbook.

The reason for this extensive influence of the Psalms on the Prayerbook is twofold: first, the Prayerbook was under the influence of the Temple in Jerusalem where psalms were chanted by the Levites every day; and secondly, the very spirit of the Psalms is so akin to the spirit of prayer that such an influence is inevitable.

The Mishnah informs us (m. Tomid VII, 3-4) that in the Temple the Levites sang a psalm at the close of each day's service. On Sunday they chanted Psalm 24, "The earth is the Lord's and the fulness thereof." On Monday they chanted Psalm 48, "Great is the Lord, and highly to be praised, in the city of our God, His holy mountain." On Tuesday they chanted Psalm 82, "God standeth in the congregation of God, in the midst of the judges, He judgeth." And so on through the week: on Wednesday, Psalm 94; on Thursday, Psalm 81; on Friday, Psalm 93; on Saturday, they chanted Psalm 92, a song for the Sabbath day, "It is a good thing to give thanks unto the Lord and to sing praises to Thy Name, O Most High."

It was natural for these Levite Psalms to have become a part of the synagogue service. As we have discussed previously, the very regularity of the daily synagogue prayer-service was derived from the regularity of the Temple sacrifice service. When the lay committees, the *Ma-a-modos*, spent their week in the Temple at Jerusalem, the people at home (in the respective districts) held daily prayers at the hours when the regular sacrifices were offered. Thus they came to feel that their prayers were the devotional counterpart of the Temple ritual (i.e., "Service of the Heart," Avodo She-ba-lev). It, therefore, seemed appropriate that the psalms which the Levites sang each day of the week in the Temple, be carried over into the corresponding days of the synagogue service week.

Besides these daily Levitical psalms, other psalms were carried over from the Temple ritual into the synagogue services. In the Temple on Passover during the slaughter of the paschal lambs, the Levites recited the group of Psalms 113-118 which are known as the Hallel Psalms, the Psalms of Praise (m. P'sochim v, 7; Tosefta P'sochim iii, 11). These psalms were then ordained for recitation in the home at the Passover meal and in the synagogue during the Passover service. Later the recitation of these Hallel Psalms spread to the other festivals.

Another group of Temple psalms which found its way into the synagogue services are

Psalms 120-134. The Mishnah (m. Suko v, 4) says that the Levites recited these fifteen psalms on the fifteen steps which led up from the Court of Women to the Court of Men. In later times, these psalms came to be used in the Sabbath Afternoon Service.

Besides the historical reason for the presence of so many psalms in the synagogue service (namely, the connection of the synagogues with the Temple), there is also a spiritual-psychological reason. The Psalms are the greatest collection of lyric poetry which came to us from antiquity. Lyric poetry is primarily an expression of the inner moods, the joys and sorrows of the poet. It is often more than that. It is generally an expression of kinship between the mood of the poet and the mood which he finds in nature. In lyric poetry the poet not only describes his own happiness but he connects his happiness with nature's joy, "Then my heart with rapture fills and dances with the daffodils," or, "I wander lonely as a cloud." Lyric poetry harmonizes the mood of man with the mood of nature. If we substitute for the term "nature" the more specific concept "God," then we find that this description of the lyric is virtually a description of prayer. Prayer is the search for harmony between man and God, the quest for communion between the finite and the Infinite. Thus it was natural that the same impulse which created the Psalm lyrics should have helped in the creation of the Prayerbook, particularly since the Psalms themselves are expressions of the communion of the psalmist with his Father in heaven. They are not only lyrical poems; they are lyrical prayers. Hence, it was no mere historic accident that the period of the development of the greater part of the Psalm-book itself should also be the period of the development of the Synagogue and the Prayerbook. The same lyrical impulse created them both.

The large proportion of the Prayerbook text which is occupied by the Psalms leads us to the conclusion that in the earliest days of its development the psalms may have constituted almost the entire bulk of the service, except, of course, for such historic sentences as, "Hear O Israel." That is to say, the people, when they gathered for the reading and study of Scripture, also recited those prayerful psalms. Certainly the psalms are among the oldest elements in the prayer ritual. The effect of the psalms upon the developing service was not only to enrich its devotional mood but also to fix its literary style. The people learned to recite those psalms which became part of the synagogue service. The texts of the psalms remained in their minds when they came to write additional prayers. Thus some of the earliest non-biblical prayers are enriched with psalm verses while others are composed entirely of scattered psalm verses and constitute virtual mosaics of psalm verses.

In addition to the use of actual psalm verses as material in the composition of prayers, the literary style of psalm poetry helped fix the style of the prayers. As is well known, the poetry of the Bible, specifically that of the psalms, does not make use of rhyme and rhythm but employs a succession of double clauses. The thought is stated in the first clause and then is repeated in different phraseology in the second clause. Thus, the thought is expressed twice in each couplet, and two by two the lines march on through the poem. This parallelism is generally a synonymous parallelism, that is to say, the thought of the first line is repeated with slight variation in the second line of the couplet. For example, Psalm 18:17:

    a) He sent from on high, He took me;
    b) He drew me out of many waters.

    a) He delivered me from mine enemy most
       strong,
    b) And from them that hated me, for they were
       too mighty for me.

This couplet style, characteristic of biblical poetry, particularly that of the Psalms, was followed in the original prayers written in the Prayerbook. As late as the middle of the talmudic epoch we find prayers still written in the couplet style of the Psalms. An examination of the older prayers will reveal the fact that in many of them (that is to say, those which are not in the fixed form of a b'rocho, a blessing) each separate thought is expressed twice in the manner of the poetic style of biblical poetry. A few examples will suffice to make this evident.

> The help of our fathers hast Thou been forever,
> In all generations a Shield and Savior to their
> sons.

> Happy the man who hearkens to Thy commands,
> And the word of Thy law he taketh to heart. . . .

> Let us adore the Lord of all
> And honor give to the world's Creator.

> The seat of His glory is in heaven above,
> The place of His power in the highest heights.

(Cf. *The Book of Psalms, A Commentary* by Solomon B. Freehof, page 6.)

Thus the biblical Psalms not only provided the earliest prayers but also taught the people of Israel how prayers should be written. They had the effect of determining the literary mood of the book of prayer in its entirety. Because of the psalm influence in direct quotation and as an example to authors of prayers, the book of prayer always remained essentially poetic. The style was thus set for all prayers. They were never to be prosaic, essay-like or solemnly didactic, but always, no matter what the theme, to be couched in the vivid imagery of poetic language. As the centuries went by this poetic influence did not die out. When, in the Middle Ages, the persecution of the Jews led to the insertion in the prayers of long historical descriptions of many persecutions and expulsions, these very plaints were put in the form of poetry. When, during the great flowering of philosophic thought (particularly in Spanish Jewry), there arose a desire to include careful philosophic descriptions of the nature of God, even these philosophic descriptions were put in the form of poetry. The famous hymns, *"Yigdal"* and *"Adon Olom,"* are philosophic definitions of God. Since they were included in the Prayerbook, they were couched in poetic form. Thus the Psalms not only determined the devotional mood of the prayers, leading them to exultant affirmations of God's goodness and grandeur, but they also set the style of the Prayerbook, making it forever poetic.

This poetic style, developed under the influence of the Psalms, had another and a correlative influence on the Prayerbook. The psalms which the Levites recited in the Temple were not really recited but were sung to musical accompaniment. The word "lyric" is related to the word "lyre" and originally referred to poems which could be sung to the accompaniment of the lyre and other instrumental music. The psalms themselves frequently speak of singing unto the Lord and make numerous references to flutes, trumpets, and string instruments.

Because of this fact the psalms made the Prayerbook not only poetic but also musical. Since it was customary to sing the psalms themselves as they appeared in the Prayerbook, it seemed natural to sing the rest of the prayers. Hence, side by side with the development of the words of the Prayerbook came the development of synagogue music. The Jewish Prayerbook gave this tone to other prayerbooks. Public prayer became a great art, combining poetry and music.

Of the large collection of psalms which are preserved in the Bible, some never appeared in the Prayerbook while others became favorite vehicles of devotions. This choice was not accidental. Some psalms became part of the service because of their association with the Temple and others because their mood expressed the predominant spirit of Jewish worship. It is of especial interest to note which of the psalms gradually found their way into the Prayerbook. In the daily service quite appropriately the morning psalms begin with Psalm 100, "Shout unto the Lord, all the earth. Serve the Lord with gladness." It then continues with Psalm 145, "I will extol Thee, my God, O King; and I will bless Thy name for ever and ever. Every day will I bless Thee; and I will praise Thy Name for ever and ever." Then the great Hallelujah Psalms from Psalm 146 to the close of the Psalter, ending with the great symphonic hymn, the 150th Psalm, concluding with the words, "Let every thing that hath breath praise the Lord. Hallelujah."

On the Sabbath, psalms are added to these Hallelujah Psalms and all in the same exultant mood. These Sabbath Psalms begin with Psalm 19, "The heavens declare the glory of God and the firmament showeth His handiwork." Then comes Psalm 34, "I will bless the Lord at all times, His praise shall continually be in my mouth." Then the great 90th Psalm, "Lord Thou hast been our dwelling-place in all generations." Then the 91st, "O Thou that dwellest in the covert of the Most High, and abidest in the shadow of the Almighty." And then two Hallelujah Psalms, 135 and 136, ending with the 33rd Psalm, "Rejoice in the Lord, O ye righteous." And special Sabbath Psalms 92 and 93, "It is a good thing to give thanks unto the Lord," and "The Lord reigneth; He is clothed in majesty."

For the festivals further on in the service, there is a special group of psalms from Psalm 113 to Psalm 118, the Hallel Psalms. The title "Hallel," which has the same root as the word "hallelujah," indicates the mood of the psalms. They are all psalms of exaltation and praise.

It is important to note that the psalms selected for the service were not the many dejected, depressed, heart-breaking psalms, with which the Psalter so touchingly abounds but rather the psalms of man's triumphant rise above the tragedy of circumstance. These psalms, recited by the people of Israel through all the vicissitudes of their long experience, indicate the heroic resolution that in spite of all suffering and tragedy, day by day we find the courage to thank the Lord for His mercy unto His children. Not only on the joyous festivals and the reposeful Sabbath, but on every day of the week through the work-a-day year, in times of grief as well as of joy, of poverty and of suffering, the psalms selected since ancient times in the Prayerbook and recited by every child of Israel, are affirmative, heroic, finding even in life's saddest days the reason and the courage for thanks and praise to God.

VI

Before Whom Thou Standest

THE SH'MA AND THE IDEA OF GOD

OLLOWING the group of psalms (P'sukei d'zimro) comes the most important part of the Morning Service, the section embodying the famous verse from Deuteronomy (6:4), "Hear, O Israel, the Lord our God, the Lord is One." This section, with the "Hear, O Israel" (Sh'ma Yisroel) as its heart and various blessings at the beginning and at the end, is the climax of the liturgy. The name of this entire section is Yotser which means "The Creator," inasmuch as it begins with a paragraph describing God as the Creator of the Universe. (*Union Prayerbook*,* Morning Service, page 119, "Praise ye the Lord . . ."; page 121, "The Holy One of Israel"; Evening Service, page 12, "Praise ye the Lord," to bottom of page 16, "Redeemer of Israel." Singer *Prayerbook*, Morning Service, pages 43-53; Evening Service, pages 129-138.)

* *Union Prayerbook*, unless otherwise indicated, refers to Newly Revised Edition of the *Union Prayerbook*, Vol. I.

This section is one of the oldest parts of the service. Just when the custom of reciting the Sh'ma Yisroel, with or without its amplifying blessings, arose, is no longer known, but certainly it is ancient. The paragraph which follows the sentence, "Hear, O Israel," in the Book of Deuteronomy determines the time of day when this prayer should be recited. It says, "These words which I command thee . . . thou shalt speak of them when thou liest down and when thou risest up." In conformity with this verse the custom arose to recite the Sh'ma at dawn and upon retiring at night. Thus the Sh'ma Yisroel is connected with the natural mode of worshipping God at the two crucial hours of the day, sunrise and sunset, and to this day is part of the Morning and Evening Services. Of course, it is still recited also before retiring at night, which was evidently its original use before it was carried over into the Sunset Service of the synagogue. The rabbis in their earliest discussions deal with the question of how to define exactly the time limits at the beginning and at the end of the day within which it was proper to recite the Sh'ma. It is easy to see, therefore, why the Sh'ma Yisroel and the blessings surrounding it gradually became part of the Morning and the Evening Services. It could not be in the Afternoon Service, since that is neither the time for "lying down" or "rising up."

The structure of this whole Yotser section, containing the Sh'ma, can best be understood when we realize the succession of ideas which it intends to convey. The very selection of this particular sentence from the Bible, "Hear O Israel, the Lord our God, the Lord is One," points to the essential and the original meaning of this whole section of the service. This sentence constitutes a descriptive definition of the nature of God. God's unity, God's uniqueness, the non-reality of all other gods worshipped, the folly of polytheism, God the only Lord of the world, the great prophetic insistence stated as clearly in this verse as in any other verse in the Bible, reveals that the purpose of this whole section is to clarify the idea of God. This purpose is made all the more evident by the invocation which opens the entire section, *"Bor'chu es adonoy ham'voroch"* (Praise ye the Lord Who is worthy of Praise). This verse, based upon Nehemiah (9:5), calls upon the people to praise God Who merits their praise; and after this invocation follow those descriptions of God's nature which show why He merits man's praise.

In other words, this whole section, the Yotser, is really theological. This fact requires some explanation. It is often stated that Judaism is not credal or theological. This is an overstatement. The more correct statement would be that the religion of Israel was not theoretical. It was not created by a series of syllogisms worked out on purely formal grounds by secluded philosophers as were, for example, the great Greek religious movements of later times, Neo-Platonism and Stoicism. The awareness and the knowledge of God in Israel was primary and natural. It grew out of the daily experience of men and women. The prophets constantly pointed to the facts of the current history of the nation, the day-by-day relationship between man and man, in the field, in the city, in commerce, and in labor. From the experience of life came the awareness of the nature of God, "O consider and see that the Lord is good" (Psalm 34:9). Therefore, while we do not have in earlier Jewish literature the type of conscious theology and scholasticism produced later by the Spanish-Jewish philosophers who endeavored to harmonize Jewish tradition with Greek and Arabic philosophy, nevertheless even the Bible discusses the nature of God. But these biblical discussions are a series of self-evident propositions derived from daily life.

That some such clear description rather than a scientific definition of God is needed in the Prayerbook is fairly obvious. It is brought out clearly in a story told in the Talmud (b. B'rochos 28b) of one of the earlier rabbis. When Rabbi Eliezer was dying his disciples gathered around him and feeling that a man at the end of his life, freed from attachments to life's vanities, is likely to see more clearly the realities of human existence, they asked, "Rabbi, teach us the path of life." He gave them many bits of sage counsel, two of which are significant for our discussion. "Keep your children from speculation; and when ye pray know before Whom ye stand." The first statement meant: do not be too greatly attracted to theoretical philosophic speculation; nevertheless, when you pray, come to a clear realization of Him in Whose presence you stand. To that great teacher, who expressed the essential mood of Judaism, a theoretic, formal theology was not needed, but a clear realization of God was nevertheless essential for genuine prayer. The nature of our prayers will depend upon our conception of God to Whom we pray. If we think of God as a warrior, our prayers are likely to be warlike. If we think of God as the average Greco-Roman thought of his gods, as no better or worse than ourselves, seeking physical indulgences and prone to jealousies, then our prayer would be a bargaining between equals as, indeed, Roman prayer generally was. Or, if we think of God as so remote and exalted as to be out of touch with human life, our prayers would shrivel away virtually to nothing. Hence, the mood and content of the whole prayer-service depend on what is contained in this section; and perhaps, too, it is the realization of the necessity of a clear idea of God before one can engage in intelligent prayer, which has resulted in the custom of having inscribed over the Holy Ark in the synagogue Rabbi Eliezer's sentence, "Know before Whom thou standest."

The first paragraph of the Yotser section, descriptive of God "to Whom we pray," speaks of Him Who brings light to the world. "How many are Thy works, Who renewest every day the works of creation, Creator of light and darkness, Who bringest peace and createst everything." The section is sealed with the benediction, "Praised be Thou, O Lord Who createth the lights." This description, based to a considerable extent on the phraseology of Isaiah (45:7), speaks of God not only as the Artist of that far-distant event, the Creation of the Universe out of chaos, but much more significantly, as the One Who re-creates the world every day, Whose presence is necessary to its maintenance, without Whose laws it would lapse into chaos again. For every night's rest and every day's dawning, for the eternal maintenance of nature's laws, for God's constant creation of the world, we offer our thanks.

The second paragraph begins with a description of God's love for His people Israel and His help to our fathers in the past. That help is manifested chiefly in the fact that God taught our fathers the laws of life because they trusted in Him. It, therefore, continues with a plea that God be our Teacher. Let us learn His law, the law of life, that we may revere Him and order our life in accordance with His law.

It will be noticed at once that the second paragraph in description of God is more specifically Jewish than the first. The idea of God as manifest in nature is universal, even to the savage who sees his gods in every natural phenomenon. But the idea of God in history, as guiding men through the mazes of their experience, is one which is much less frequently found in the history of religion. The concept of God as the Lord of time as well as the Lord of space is not a usual one, and the specific idea of what God has achieved in history is hardly found elsewhere, namely, that God is the great Teacher, that it is He Who has implanted in the human heart the desire to learn and Who is now asked to teach us to be His disciples and to learn His ways. This idea could only have arisen among a people who had learned the joy of democratic education and who, at times, pictured heaven itself as a great academy and God as the great Instructor.

The logic of the sequence of thought, God as Creator and God as Teacher, the Universe and the Torah, lies in the fact that God's control of the Universe has the greater bearing upon human life the more that man is intelligently aware of God's presence and work in the world. Both these ideas are combined in Psalm 19. The Psalm begins with a description of God the Creator, "The heavens declare the glory of God," and ends with a paean of praise for the Torah, "The Law of the Lord is perfect, restoring the soul."

After these two blessings, God the Creator and God the Teacher, comes the great sentence, "Hear O Israel, the Lord our God, the Lord is One." In the early days of the struggle against actual polytheism this sentence must have meant primarily a denial of idolatry. But through the ages its psychological effect was to summarize and climax the two preceding blessings. It expressed the idea that, whether you are moved by the miracle of nature or by the grandeur of history, whether you think in terms of space or of time, whether you think of the wonders of the natural world or of the upward struggle of man, through whatever avenue of wonder and understanding God enters your heart, "The Lord our God is One." All human concepts of God are but fragments of the Infinite unity.

Following the sentence, "Hear O Israel," comes the paragraph which follows in Deuteronomy, "Thou shalt love the Lord thy God with

· 66 ·

all thy heart." It is strange that the mood of Judaism has been so persistently misunderstood. The God Whom Israel worships has been frequently described as a harsh, terrifying judge Who threatens His children with dire punishment, and allegiance to Whom is rooted in terror. The "God of the Old Testament" is always contrasted with the "God of the New Testament," Who is described as loving and tender. It is, of course, true that the Old Testament, preserving many ideas from many periods in religious evolution, contains both harsh and tender ideas. Nor is the New Testament free from stern imprecations. The important question is: which of the many God-conceptions found in the Old Testament had actual influence over the life of the Jewish people? In what terms did Israel think of God? The answer is clear.

Of all the descriptions of God and of man's relationship to Him, the people of Israel selected for the very center and climax of the Prayerbook none of the sterner descriptions, not the command to dread God's punishment but, "Thou shalt love the Lord thy God with all thy heart." That was the concept of the relationship between the human and the divine which the founders of the synagogue found most significant in the Bible and which they placed centrally in the Prayerbook to be a day-by-day

· 67 ·

influence upon the lives of the people of Israel. Although the Bible necessarily contains many ideas of God, the Prayerbook, the living expression of the faith of Israel, comes to its climax with the idea of God Whom we must love with all our heart. Thus, after the description of God as the Creator and God as the Teacher, comes the sense of God the Friend. The Prayerbook here expresses the traditional symbolic interpretation of the sentence in the Song of Songs, "I am my Beloved's and He is mine" (Song of Songs 6:3). The entire section closes with a final blessing which is called the Redemption (*G'ulo*). (*Union Prayerbook*, Morning Service, page 120, "True and enduring," to page 125, "Praised be Thou, our Redeemer, the Holy One of Israel"; Evening Service, page 14, "Eternal Truth," to page 16, "Praised be Thou, O Lord, Redeemer of Israel." Singer *Prayerbook*, Morning Service, page 51, "True and firm," to page 53, "Blessed art Thou, O Lord, Who hast redeemed Israel"; Evening Service, page 134, "True and trustworthy," to page 136, "Blessed art Thou . . . Who guardest Thy people Israel for ever.")

This section in the Morning and Evening Services in all rituals begins with an affirmation of faith. The worshiper declares the truth that God is the Maintainer of the world, the Teacher of the human mind and heart, He Whom we love with all our heart and soul; we know that this is true because of His redemption of Israel from Egypt.

The redemption from Egypt is constantly referred to in the Prayerbook. In the Kiddush, the wine ceremony ushering in not only the Passover, which specifically commemorates that deliverance, but every festival and even the Sabbath each week, the phrase, "A remembrance of the Exodus from Egypt," is used. Every man in every generation is asked to look upon himself as though he personally came out of Egypt. All social legislation, frowning upon the permanent slavery common to mankind in every civilization and calling for the liberation of every child of Israel who is held by his brothers as a slave, is based upon the fact, as the rabbis explain it, that we are servants of God and must not be slaves of man. To enjoy liberty is not only the privilege of every child of God but also his duty. The story of the deliverance from Egypt, recited twice every day in the Prayerbook, helped the worshipers maintain their courage to live. For God's destruction of Pharaoh's tyranny was symbolic to the rabbis of the hope that all such tyrannies, however powerful, would be overthrown and all who were oppressed and persecuted would be redeemed. No power on earth is equal to the majestic power of God Himself.

Hence, in this section the phrase from the song which Israel sang at the shore of the Red Sea is prominently quoted: "Who is like unto Thee among the mighty, O Lord, Who is like unto Thee, glorious in holiness, working wonders." On the basis of that ancient experience the rabbis founded their hope of redemption from every tragedy, and implicit in that hope was the assurance of mankind restored to liberty from every oppression. The *Union Prayerbook* phrases clearly the idea implicit in the entire prayer when it gives the following version of the close of the blessing (page 16), "As Thou hast redeemed Israel and saved him from arms stronger than his own, so mayest Thou redeem all who are oppressed and persecuted. Praised be Thou O Lord, Redeemer of Israel."

This, then, is the concept of God which dominates the Prayerbook. Philosophers might think of other attributes which they would be inclined to deem essential. Theologians might wish to include much more in order to present a complete creed. Bible students might discover other descriptions of God which this Prayerbook picture does not include. But the God-concept as selected and developed and emphasized in this Prayerbook section (Yotser) was the effective God-concept through all the centuries of Israel's devotional prayer. When Israel sought in the

Prayerbook to clarify the idea of Him before Whom they stood when they prayed, they hailed Him twice daily as the Creator and Maintainer of nature, the Guide and Teacher of man, the Friend Who is to be loved with all our heart and soul, and the Great Redeemer Who overthrows every Pharaoh and brings His children to liberty and peace.

VII

I Will Arrange My Prayer

THE T'FILO AND THE IDEA OF PRAYER

> If on a spring night I went by,
> And God were standing there,
> What is the prayer that I should cry
> To Him? This is the prayer:
> O Lord of Courage grave
> O Master of this night of spring
> Make firm in me a heart too brave
> To ask Thee anything.

THE poet-novelist Galsworthy thus expressed his philosophy of prayer. He voices a widespread feeling that "to ask God for anything" is rather unworthy. There is a definite distaste on the part of many people for the petitional type of prayer. Some feel, as does Galsworthy, that it is somehow cowardly to beg for favors. Others say that it is futile to expect Infinity to heed our little petitions.

It is interesting to note that the deprecation of petitional prayer is not necessarily a product of religious doubt. It is found in the Bible; it is implied in the Talmud and is inherent in the

Prayerbook itself. The Prophet Isaiah (65:17-25) described the blessed era of the future when God will establish "a new heaven and a new earth." He visualized the ideal time when man will not need to make much use of petitional prayer. "Before they call, I will answer, and while they are yet speaking, I will hear" (Isa. 65:24). So, too, Ecclesiastes (5:1) counsels, "Let not thy heart be hasty to utter a word before God . . . let thy words be few." The same deprecation of incessant petitioning is found in the New Testament (Matt. 6:7, 8), "But when ye pray, use not vain repetitions, as the heathens do . . . for your Father knoweth what things ye have need of, before ye ask Him." The prayer of Rabbi Eliezer, to be uttered in time of peril, avoids specific petitions and merely asks that God's will be done. "Do Thy will in the heavens above. Give serenity of soul to those who revere Thee and do what is good in Thy sight" (b. B'rochos 29b).

The same tendency to limit the amount of petitioning is evident in the Prayerbook itself. The very construction of the service is evidence of this fact. It will be noted that in the first two major sections of the daily service, namely, in the Chapters of Song (P'sukei d'zimro) and in the Sh'ma (or Yotser), there are almost no prayers which contain pleas or petitions. The only petition comes in the closing phrase of the Sh'ma, which asks God to redeem the oppressed, and this is merely the conclusion of the blessing describing God as the Deliverer from Egypt.

Yet for all this, it is difficult to conceive of sincere prayer without some petitions for blessing and pleas for Divine favor. God in Judaism (and later in Christianity) is thought of as our Father. This intimate relationship inevitably affects the mood and content of prayer. It is an unworthy child who nags his father with incessant demands, but it is natural for a child to look to his father for guidance and help. When Galsworthy wants to be "too brave to ask for anything," he is going in the right direction—but too far! As a matter of fact, he does make a petitional prayer: asking that God grant him a "firm" and steadfast heart. In the Prayerbook, the first two sections (the Psalms of Praise and the Sh'ma), contain virtually no petitions, but the third section, which now follows, is devoted to petitional prayers. Yet even in this section the petitions are limited by certain definite and significant restrictions which in themselves indicate the Jewish ideal of petitional prayer.

This petitional part of the daily public prayer is known by three different names. It is called the Sh'mone Esre, which means "eighteen" and refers to the eighteen petitional blessings which it originally contained (now there are nineteen but the ancient name still is used). Secondly, it is called the T'filo, which means the "petitional prayer," derived from the root which means "to judge," and is an appeal to God, the Judge, to help us. And thirdly, it is called Amida, which means the "standing" prayer, referring to the fact that the worshiper must stand while reciting this part of the service.

(*Union Prayerbook*, page 124, beginning with "Praised be Thou, O Lord, God of our fathers"; page 140, "Praised be Thou O Lord, Giver of peace." Also, page 320, "Praised be Thou O Lord, God of our fathers," to page 324, "Giver of peace." Singer *Prayerbook*, page 53, "Blessed art Thou, O Lord our God and God of our fathers," to page 66, "Blessed art Thou, O Lord, Who blessest Thy people Israel with peace.")

This group of nineteen benedictions, the petitional prayer, is recited three times a day, morning, afternoon, and evening. Thus, it differs from the Sh'ma with its benedictions which, being linked to sunrise and sunset, is recited only twice a day, at the Morning and Evening Services. The Morning and the Evening Services have both the Sh'ma and the T'filo, while the Afternoon Service has only the T'filo.

Why was this group of prayers recited at each

of the three services during the day? As stated in Chapter v, the rabbis have a number of theories. One is that the T'filos were ordained to correspond to the regular offerings of the Temple. This theory explained the Morning T'filo as corresponding with the morning burnt-offering and the Afternoon T'filo as corresponding with the regular afternoon burnt-offering, but there was no regular offering to which the Evening Service, specifically the Evening T'filo, corresponded. There was no night service in the Temple. Therefore, they said, the Evening T'filo corresponded to the burning of the fat and the limbs of the offering which burned all night. Since there was no actual service in the Temple at night, and therefore, no real parallel for the T'filo in our Evening Services, it is evident that the T'filo was not originally a part of the Evening Service. This is substantiated today by the fact that, whereas the T'filos in the Morning and Afternoon Services are read silently by each worshiper and then are recited aloud by the cantor, the T'filo in the Evening Service is not recited aloud by the cantor at all.

Each T'filo has three main divisions: the three introductory blessings, the thirteen intervening blessings (on Sabbath and festivals only one intervening blessing), and the three concluding blessings. Whether it be a T'filo for the daily service or for the Sabbath or for the holidays, the three introductory blessings and the three concluding blessings are always the same. The difference is only with regard to the intervening blessing or blessings. The only exception being the T'filos on the New Year and the Day of Atonement in which the third introductory blessing is somewhat amplified. On week-days there are thirteen intervening blessings; therefore, the T'filo has nineteen (originally eighteen) benedictions. On the Sabbath and festivals there is only one intervening blessing, referring specifically to the occasion; and, therefore, the T'filo consists of seven blessings. However, in the Musof of the New Year, because of the blowing of the Shofor, there are three intervening blessings, therefore, that T'filo is exceptionally a nine-blessing T'filo.

Although the T'filo contains most of the petitional prayers found in the entire service, the three opening and three concluding blessings which are common to the T'filo of the week-day, Sabbath, and festival, are not petitional in their nature. The first of the three introductory blessings praises God as God of the patriarchs and ends with the words, "Praised be Thou O God, Shield of Abraham." The second speaks of God as Master of life and death and ends in the Orthodox ritual with, "Praised be Thou O

Lord Who revivest the dead." In the Reform ritual, the idea of immortality is substituted for the idea of resurrection with the words, "Praised be Thou Who hast implanted within us immortal life." The third introductory blessing speaks of God's holiness and contains the K'dusho, an elaboration of the description in Isaiah (6), where the angels call to one another in God's praise, "Holy, Holy, Holy is the Lord of Hosts." The three concluding blessings are blessings of thanks. The first asks God to accept our prayers. The second voices gratitude for God's bountiful providence to us. The third is a prayer for peace, "Grant us peace, etc."

The intervening blessings on week-days deal with a variety of actual petitions: for knowledge, for forgiveness, for help in our affliction, for healing, a blessing for the year and its produce, for Israel's deliverance, for a restoration of the judges, and prayers for the restoration of Jerusalem and the dynasty of David. Some of these prayers were changed in tone and content in the Reform ritual as will be discussed later.

Jewish literature at the time when the T'filo and the main prayers were developed, was not directly theological or theoretically philosophical, and, therefore, does not contain any systematic discussion of the nature and meaning of prayer. There are, of course, a number of scattered statements by various rabbis on this theme. These statements and particularly the analysis of the implications involved in the construction and the wording of the T'filo, will reveal the mood and something of the philosophy of prayer inherent in Judaism.

It is noteworthy that the three introductory prayers, those of the patriarchs and the prayers for God's power over life and death and God's holiness, are not petitions at all, but descriptive praises of God. Further, it should be noted that all of the petitions of the intervening part of the T'filo are couched in the form of a blessing, always ending with the words, "Praised be Thou O God." The fact that even the petitions are also praises of God and, therefore, not exclusively or even predominantly petitional in mood, clearly reveals a significant attitude toward prayer itself as a spiritual exercise. This attitude has been specifically stated in the following rabbinic statement, "A man should always utter the praises of God before he offers his petitions" (b. B'rochos 32a). Judging by this mood in the T'filo, prayer is primarily the achievement of an affirmative relationship to God, a sense of gratitude and appreciation for the blessings we have received. If our faith can succeed in curing us of the mood of constant discontent and can teach us to find joyous gratitude in whatever happiness we already have, however small it may be, then it will engender a healthy-mindedness within us that makes for a happy life, itself the answer to most of our prayers. This habit of praising God rather than begging from Him has become, through centuries of this type of prayer, a prevalent state of mind which enabled our fathers to find joy even in minor blessings and thus played its part in preserving Israel through the vicissitudes of history. A poverty-stricken, forlorn, exiled Jew, raising his last crust of bread to his mouth might perhaps be justified in cursing his lot and denouncing God, but instead it would not enter his mind to partake of this bit of bread without first saying, "Praised be Thou O Lord Who bringest forth food from the earth." The rabbis speak even of a higher state of heroism, a more triumphant conquest of bitterness when they say, "A man should praise God even for misfortunes as much as he praises Him for happiness" (m. B'rochos ix, 5). Whether this lofty courage is attainable by the average Jew or not, he learns to feel and to express, or perhaps to express and thus to feel, a constant sense of gratitude to the Master of the Universe. Prayer in Israel teaches man to overcome bitterness and self-pity; to think not of what the world owes *him*, but what he owes the world and God. It is not primarily piteous pleading but is essentially grateful communion with the Infinite.

The three introductory blessings of the T'filo are not only praises of God, they are also descriptions of Him. That, too, is significant, for the appreciation of the Prayerbook's idea of prayer. How we pray, why we pray, what we ask for, depends upon our understanding of the nature of God to Whom we offer our prayers. The first of the three introductory prayers, which speak of God Who showed His lovingkindness to the patriarchs, the "Shield of Abraham," indicates that with us prayer is predicated upon God's lovingkindness "known of old." We do not pray to a stern master, pleading for mercy. We are not terrified "sinners in the hand of an angry God," but we turn to Him Who bestows lovingkindness and remembers the goodness of the fathers and bringest redemption to their children in love. Our attitude in prayer must be that of a trusting child toward a loving father whose kindnesses are well remembered and to whom we turn in confidence today and in the future.

The second of the three introductory prayers speaks of God's might and His power over life and death, "Who supportest the fallen, and healest the sick and freest the imprisoned." God, the Lord of Life, mighty to save, must be vivid in the mind of everyone who prays to Him. He is the Lord of nature, omnipotent; nothing is too difficult for Him to achieve. If puny man can manipulate the fragmentary laws of nature which his dim intellect discovers and by use of these fragments of laws, half-understood, bring food to the hungry and healing to the sick, how much more then can the Master of nature "support the fallen, heal the sick, and break the chains of the captives." God is not only He Who has shown His love to our fathers, but He Who, revealing His might over life and nature, gives us assurance in our prayers to Him.

The third of the introductory blessings involves another element in the Jewish concept of prayer. It reads, "Thou art Holy, Thy Name is Holy. . . . Praised be Thou O God of Holiness." The holiness of God, the supreme statement of the moral nature of the Divine, is a basic concept in Judaism and has an important bearing on the whole conception of prayer. God's holiness, which means God's supreme ethical perfection, implies that to Him the ill-used may confidently turn for justice and the persecuted for mercy. Among no pagan nation whose gods were pictured as pleasure-loving, mutually jealous and brutal, could prayer ever rise to so noble a height. It is only the consciousness that the Universe is dominated by a Holy God, by a justice without flaw, a mercy without stint, a goodness without limit, which can give to the heart-broken and the forlorn one final court of appeal. God's holiness is the last fortress of the persecuted and the oppressed.

This concept of the Divine Holiness, without which the unfortunate would be left bereft of hope forever, received further development in the Prayerbook. The holiness of God became the sun to which every human soul like an earth-born plant raises itself to flower and fruit. God's holiness is not merely a splendor, distant and unattainable, but a light, absorbed and reflected and sought for in every human life. This was already expressed in the Bible (Lev. 19:2), "Ye shall be holy; for I the Lord your God am holy." In this third blessing of the T'filo, the human striving for holiness in imitation of God is poetically depicted in the elaboration of the text. When the reader repeats the T'filo and comes to this blessing the congregation and the reader unite in the special praise of God's Holiness, called the K'dusho, the Sanctification. The K'dusho is based upon the sixth chapter of Isaiah where, in the prophet's vision, the angels call to one another and say, "Holy, Holy, Holy, is the Lord of Hosts, the whole earth is filled with His glory." But here in the Prayerbook this idea receives a beautiful amplification. It is not only the angels, conceived as celestial beings, pure and without sin, who thus chant the holiness of God, but, "*we* sanctify Thy Name on earth as the heavens declare Thy glory" (*Union Prayerbook*, page 126). The songs of the angels and the thoughts of man, the music of the spheres and the hymns of earth-bound beings, join in praising the holiness of God.

These three blessings constitute the preparation for prayer, and this spiritual preparation constitutes one of its chief blessings, for prayer is a hallowing of the personality. We pray in order to lift our hearts to God, to have Him enter our minds and our consciousness, to live in His presence, to partake of the light of His holiness, and in that communion to grow cleaner of heart and stronger in spirit. The three blessings bring a sense of the appreciation of whatever joys we have as voiced in praises of God, an awareness of God as the loving Father Who has shown His lovingkindness to our forebears in ages past, a confidence in His might as Master of nature, and an ennoblement of our own soul by joining all nature in praise of His holiness.

With this mood re-created daily by the very introduction of the T'filo, the various actual petitions enumerated above can be uttered with pure heart. And even these petitions themselves indicate an additional attitude of the Prayerbook with regard to petitional prayer. All those petitions which follow the introductory three, are in the plural. The sick do not ask, "Grant me healing," but, "Heal us, O Lord." The text of the prayer is based upon the verse in Jeremiah (17:14) which reads, "Heal me, O Lord, and I shall be healed." But the Prayerbook changes the biblical text from singular to plural. The afflicted say, "See *our* affliction." And so through all the prayers.

While there is ample provision later on in the service for whatever individual and personal needs a man may have for his own welfare, part of the training in prayer is the sense of community. In the midst of our own affliction we gather with our fellows and think of their sorrows, too. Not only is our burden thereby lightened as we are thus redeemed from self-centered self-torture, but there is created in us a sense of human unity, the fellowship of pain, the fraternity of suffering.

This social-spiritual ideal of "enlarging the tent" of our spirit to include all who are in sadness and in pain, was specifically expressed as a principle of prayer in one of the dicta of the rabbis (b. B'rochos 30a), "A man must always unite himself with the congregation when he prays." Another talmudic statement reads, "Whoever prays in behalf of his fellowmen, his prayer is answered first" (b. Bovo Kamo 92a).

After the various petitions, the T'filo ends with the three concluding blessings. The first is a general petition that God accept our prayers; then follows a prayer of thanks for God's daily providence, and finally a prayer for peace, "Grant us peace, etc." Originally the daily T'filo ended with the priestly blessing, "The Lord bless thee, and keep thee, etc." (Num. 6:24-26). This blessing concludes with the words, "and grant thee peace." The present closing benediction, "Grant us peace," is an elaboration of the final words of the priestly blessing and forms a fitting conclusion to the entire T'filo. It implies that prayer should be so ordered and so uttered as to bless the worshiper with a spirit of peace. Whether his petitions are granted or not, will depend upon God's will and His knowledge of what is for our good. The T'filo ends in the mood of Rabbi Eliezer's prayer, which was quoted at the beginning of this chapter, "Do Thy will in the heavens above. Grant serenity of soul to those who revere Thee; and do what is good in Thy sight."

The entire T'filo is an exemplification of the Jewish ideal of prayer. Its opening paragraphs of praise prepare the heart to conquer resentment and bitterness and to find happiness in the blessings already received. The intervening petitions, couched in the plural, teach the individual to make his life unselfish, to think of the needs and the sorrows of his fellow man. The concluding benedictions end with the note of social and personal peace which comes from the sense of communion with God.

This Jewish ideal of prayer is expressed in many statements in the Talmud. These statements may not have been familiar to the average worshiper but their spirit was inherent in the very structure and wording of the T'filo. The worshiper was not a philosopher or a theologian, yet a definite theology of prayer, a mood of gratitude, faith, and self-ennoblement, was developed in him as day by day he read at home or in the synagogue the historic T'filo.

VIII

Commune with Your Heart

TACHANUN AND PRIVATE DEVOTION

IMMEDIATELY after the close of the petitional prayers, the T'filo, there is a prayer for silent devotion, beginning "O God, keep my tongue from evil and my lips from speaking guile" (*Union Prayerbook*, page 140; Singer *Prayerbook*, page 66). This prayer is meant for personal, private devotion. It is a fitting introduction for the group of personal prayers which follows. It calls for modesty and humility and for the readiness to forgive all who offend against us. The Talmud (b. B'rochos 16b to 17a), which is the original source of this prayer, has a number of similar prayers each one of which has the heading: "Rabbi . . . . . . after saying the T'filo said the following." All of the prayers are personal devotions, expressing individual moods and needs. In some of the older rituals most of these prayers of the rabbis were placed after the T'filo to be recited by those who wished to use them. Later on, all but this one dropped out, and other prayers of personal and penitential nature took their place. This whole section for personal prayer is called "The Tachanun," which means "supplication" (in the Singer *Prayerbook* up to page 80).

The purpose of this part of the service is to provide an opportunity for personal devotion; as the rabbis phrase it, to ask "for one's own needs." There is considerable discussion in talmudic literature as to just where in the service one should insert his own personal petitions to God, in addition to those petitions (described in the preceding chapter) which were uttered in behalf of the community. Some say that each man could amplify the various blessings of the T'filo by adding his personal prayers. Some say that in the prayer of the T'filo which begins, "Hear our voice," a man may add his personal devotions. But it finally became established that the personal devotions should be added at the close of the T'filo where a man could pray as long as he wished without delaying the congregational prayer. Evidently, by the time of the composition of those personal prayers which are mentioned in the Talmud (b. B'rochos 16b to 17a), the custom of reciting private supplications after the T'filo was fairly well established. It is noteworthy that from the beginning the very scholars who were careful to fix the exact rules and regulations for public prayer were just as careful to foster private and personal prayer. Careful provision is made in talmudic literature for private prayers to be added to the regular public prayers. It was, indeed, considered a man's duty to add something new to his regular daily prayer, something original and personal (j. B'rochos IV, 8a). The rabbis understood why it was necessary to insist upon these spontaneous expressions of devotion. Rabbi Eliezer (the same sage who on his death-bed warned his disciples always to realize clearly before Whom they stand in prayer), said that if a man looks upon his prayers as merely a fixed task his prayers can never be true supplication (m. B'rochos IV, 4). Words recited habitually soon are recited mechanically and the noblest liturgy may become a mere formality.

The very fact that those men who developed the Prayerbook were careful to provide ample opportunity in public ritual for private and personal devotion indicated clearly that they were well aware of this danger. They understood that the meaningfulness of public prayers must be constantly renewed by the personal sense of religious devotion and the personal practice of private prayer. Without private prayer the public service would gradually grow remote from the personal life of the average individual; but as long as the individual himself sought God in time of his own trouble and of joy, he brought to the public prayer a devoted spirit, and the synagogue became a community of spiritualized personalities. Public prayer draws its vitality from private devotion.

Magnificent as was the great sacrificial ritual in Jerusalem, it could not avoid becoming a formality in time. It was in the hands of the priests; the people participated merely as observers and uttered some pious phrases. It is true that the Pharisees, trying to democratize and personalize Judaism, attempted to stress the participation of the average Israelite in the ritual of the Temple, and it is true, likewise, that at certain parts of the daily sacrificial ritual the people present prostrated themselves and prayed to God. But the ritual itself could only be conducted by a priest and could not derive new strength from a similar private service in the life of the average Israelite. But the prayer-service, requiring no special group of men to conduct it and no particular place for its expression, achieved a constantly renewed intensity from the private devotion of spiritually-minded men and women.

As we follow the history of prayer in Israel, we find many successive periods of renewed prayerfulness among private individuals, special devotions self-imposed, especial fervor in the utterance of prayers at home, along the road, and in the forest and field; we find a sweet child-to-father informality, expressed in different lands at different times. All these flowerings of private devotion brought new life to the synagogue service and saved it from formalism. When, for example, in the sixteenth century, the mystic movement, centering in Safed, Palestine, brought an intensified sense of the intimate communion of man with God, this personal devotion imme-diately brought new prayers into the Prayer-book and new vitality into public worship. The same phenomenon occurred when the popular, mystic chasidic movement began to develop in the eighteenth century. This brought first a joy-ous personal piety and soon a renewed sincerity in public devotion.

One of the remarkable devotional results of the Cabalistic movement was the tremendous spread of prayers in Judeo-German to be used in the private devotions of pious men and women. How real and how personal some of these six-teenth and seventeenth century prayers were can be seen from the following typical examples. This is a prayer by a wife for her husband which reveals the daily life of the German Jews in those centuries and their chief occupation, travel-ling through the villages of Germany engaged in petty trade. "Deliver me, my husband and my children and all of Israel from the hands of the cruel ones and from all evil imprisonments." Or this one: "May he be delivered on his journey from all trouble and from all evil misfortunes which frequently come. I beseech Thee, dear God, protect my husband against all false accusations that he may be preserved on his journeying against the terrors of the world." The terrors of their world, the poor Jew travelling through unruly villages, the butt of coarse and cruel jests, the legitimate prey of men of violence, all leave their traces in these intimate private utterances. Because these prayers sprung from a true sense of God's presence they often rose to a simple, unstudied beauty as, for example: "Truly O Lord before Thee there is no night; light resteth with Thee. Thou givest light to the world with Thy radiance. The morning speaks of Thy grace and the night utters Thy truth. And all creatures speak of Thy love and Thy wonders, O Lord, Who renewest Thy help every day."

The New Year prayers, splendid as is their classic eloquence, are immeasurably enriched by such simple private devotions as these: "Lord of all worlds, I have come before Thee in prayer, sighing and weeping before Thy great Name. . . . Woe unto me for the evil deeds which I have done, through my bitter sins I have burdened and stained my soul which cometh from on high and which Thou hast given me to keep beautiful as a precious jewel. Lord of all worlds, have pity on me, hear the prayer which I utter with tears and with broken heart; forgive my sins, merciful Father; pity me as a father pitieth his children and inscribe me and my children and all of Israel for life and peace in the coming year so that we may be able to hallow Thy Name." Such intense emotion, the spiritual creativeness of private prayers, were the living fountains which kept the stream of Israel's devotion fresh and strong.

·IX·

Nor Can the Ignorant Be Pious

THE SCRIPTURE AND THE IDEAL OF CULTURE

OLLOWING the personal devotion, the Tachanun, is the final part of the daily Morning Service, namely, the public reading
from Scripture. The Scripture is read publicly
on the Sabbath, on the holidays, and a minor
portion is also read on Sabbath afternoon and
on Monday and Thursday mornings. Mondays
and Thursdays were market days in Palestine.
The people gathered from the villages and the
farms; hence the court convened on those days.
Extra prayers are still recited in the Tachanun
and the Scripture is read.

The practice of regular reading of Scripture
was totally unprecedented in the history of religion. The sacred books among other faiths
were secret books and restricted to the learned
few among the priests. To make such books accessible to the average Jew was not only to
democratize Judaism but to initiate in the world

the first public education. Josephus (Contra Apionem II, 18), in defending Judaism against Apion, points out this unique characteristic of Judaism and, speaking of the Law, says: "(Moses) the Law-giver demonstrated the Law to be the best and the most necessary instruction, permitting the people to leave off their other appointments and assemble together for hearing the Law and learning it exactly, and this not once or twice or oftener, but every week, which all other legislators seem to have neglected." In other words, Josephus made it clear to his Greek and Roman readers that no legislator among any other people thought of doing what Moses ordained, namely, to set aside one day of rest from labor on which the people would be free to study the Law. So, too, in Josephus (Antiquities Book XVI, II, 3), "And the seventh day be set apart from labor; it is dedicated to the learning of our customs and laws." It is to be noticed that the practice of reading the Scriptures regularly is thus ascribed to Moses. This idea is found also in the Hebrew sources. The Book of Deuteronomy requires that every seventh year the entire Law shall be read to the people (Deut. 31:10, 11). Tradition ascribes to Moses the ordinance that the Law be read on the Sabbath and holidays (b. Megillah 32a and j. Megillah IV, 1 [75a]). But this tradition merely indicates the consciousness that the institution was very old and of great authority and significance.

Parallel with the reading from the Five Books of Moses (the Law, the Torah) there is, each week, a reading from the Prophets, connected in some way either by similarity of phrases or by similarity of thought to the reading from the Torah. The prophetical readings were of ancient origin. During the Exile the people gathered words of comfort from prophets who lived among them. In all likelihood, they heard readings from the Scrolls of the writings of the other prophets of past generations. It is to be assumed, for example, that the writings of Jeremiah, recorded by his secretary and friend Baruch, were read. Jeremiah was the contemporary of these exiles and his writings, not appreciated during the days of the war, were doubly meaningful in the time of the post-war tragedy. Which of the two, Torah or Prophet, first attained the status of public reading, or just when the public reading became regular, we do not know. But this is certain, that fairly early in the period of the Second Commonwealth, the people gathered on the Sabbath and on holidays to hear the Law and the Prophets read to them.

There is a difference in the system of reading from the Books of the Law and the Books of the

Prophets. The Law was read consecutively, the section for one week following immediately the section of the preceding week. Thus, within a certain time the entire text of the Five Books of Moses was completed and the cycle then begun over again. But the reading from the prophetical books was not consecutive at all, but selective. The prophetical readings were chosen to fit, in some way, the week's selection from the Torah scroll. Thus it came about that certain sections of the Prophets were never read while other sections became quite familiar to the people.

Some scholars believe that, since the Mosaic Law required that the whole Law be read once every seventh year, the sabbatical year, that in the intervening years the five books were so divided that it would be read completely in that period. Thus, there was a seven-year cycle of readings. Others say that the Torah was so divided that it would be read through twice in the seven-year period. Thus, there would be a three-and-a-half-year cycle of reading. It is, however, a known fact that in Palestine, in Egypt, and in other lands, there was a three-year cycle for the reading of the Five Books of Moses. Corresponding to the three-year cycle, there were over one hundred and fifty special prophetical readings, each one suited to its respective scriptural reading.

The modern custom of having the Five Books of Moses divided into larger sections so that it can be read entirely in the annual cycle, comes from Babylon. It may be that the three-year cycle was condensed into a one-year cycle because the sections in the three-year cycle were too small, and perhaps also because the rabbis wanted the people to read the Law more frequently and thus know it better.

The reading of Scripture, Law, and Prophets, was from the very beginning of practical intent and practical value. It was never meant to be a mere liturgical solemnity, but as Josephus correctly says, it was for the specific purpose of instruction. This instruction was carefully and intelligently carried out. First of all, people were called up from the congregation to read portions of the Law. Nowadays the people who are called up merely recite a blessing before and after the reading of the respective subdivisions of the weekly portions, but originally each person had to read the section himself. This made it necessary for the members of the congregation to learn the reading of the Law. The Synagogue sought to develop a people of readers and students. 5 2 7 4 5

It was not merely that people had to study in order to be able to take their turn in reading the Law, but the public reading itself was an effective means of group instruction. The Law was read, verse by verse, and then translated by a trained translator into Aramaic, the language of every-day life. Then, there was an interpreter who interpreted all the implications of the passage, whether legal, describing what additional legislation was derived from the written text, or ethical, emphasizing the moral lessons which the verses implied. Thus, the sermon arose either as a legal discourse or a moral homily. The sermon, that vital expression in Judaism and in its daughter-religion, which keeps religion alive to the problems of the day and blends the past with the present, is thus derived from reading and interpreting the Law in the Jewish service. The growth and the spread of Christianity would have been unthinkable without this synagogue-born sermon.

The whole system of Scriptural reading and interpretation was carried over into the Christian church. Since the early Christians still attended the synagogue, they realized the value of the scriptural reading. Thus there grew up in the various national branches of the Christian church the regular reading of the Prophets, the Epistles, and the Gospels. Some of the national churches developed a continuous reading of the New Testament, equivalent to the Jewish consecutive reading of the Torah (Lectua Continua). As was the custom in the synagogue this continuous reading was interrupted only by special readings for the festivals. The church also adopted the custom of providing an oral translation as the Scripture was being read and also of interpreting the text, which, of course, was in Greek. While in the western half of the Roman Empire the Greek was understood when read, in the eastern half it was translated into Syriac, the language of the people. (As to the direct spiritual effect of this reading, see Hasting's *Encyclopedia of Religion and Ethics*, II, 601 ff.; and Kohler in the *Jewish Encyclopedia*, "Law-Reading," VII, 647 ff.)

Not only the reading of the Law and its interpretation but the very selection of the prophetical reading to accompany the reading each week from the Torah aroused the attention of the listeners and helped awaken the potential reasoning power in their minds. For example, for the Sabbath on which the first section from Leviticus is read, the section which describes in detail the sacrifices to be offered in the Tabernacle and later in the Temple, the selected prophetical reading is from Isaiah (43), beginning with verse 23, in which the Prophet contrasts mere ritual with God's ethical commandments. The Prophet says, "I have not burdened thee with a meal-offering, nor wearied thee with frankincense . . . but thou hast burdened Me with thy sins. Thou hast wearied Me with thine iniquities. . . . Thy first father sinned, and thine intercessors have transgressed against Me. Therefore, I have profaned the princes of the sanctuary, and I have given Jacob to condemnation, and Israel to reviling." Similarly, the following week, the reading from the Torah (Lev. 6-8) continues with the details of the sacrificial cult; therefore, the traditional reading from the Prophets is from the Prophet Jeremiah (7:21 ff.) in which the Prophet directly says: "Thus saith the Lord of Hosts, the God of Israel: Add your burnt-offerings unto your sacrifices, and eat ye flesh. For I spoke not unto your fathers, nor commanded them in the day that I brought them out of the land of Egypt, concerning burnt-offerings or sacrifices; but this thing I commanded them, saying: 'Hearken unto My voice, and I will be your God, and ye shall be My people; and walk ye in all the way that I command you, that it may be well with you.'"

An equally startling contrast is to be found in the traditional reading for the Day of Atonement itself. The reading from the Torah is taken from the sixteenth chapter of the Book of Leviticus, in which all the details of the sacrificial ritual for that Holy Day are carefully enumerated. But strangely enough, the prophetical reading, taken from Isaiah (58:2 ff.), is one in which the Prophet seems to scorn the ritual of the day and mock the people for their fasting. "They ask of Me righteous ordinances, they delight to draw near unto God. 'Wherefore have we fasted, and Thou seest not? Wherefore have we afflicted our soul, and Thou takest no knowledge?' . . . Is such a fast that I have chosen? The day for a man to afflict his soul? Is it to bow down his head as a bulrush, and to spread sackcloth and ashes under him? Wilt thou call this a fast, and an acceptable day to the Lord? Is not this the fast that I have chosen? To loose the fetters of wickedness, to undo the bands of the yoke. . . ."

These three examples carefully chosen by those who selected the prophetical reading must have raised disturbing questions in the minds of those who listened to them on the Sabbath and on the holidays. The mood of the prophetical reading seems to be so different from the mood of the reading from the Torah as virtually to contradict it. It was almost as if the readings were selected to shock worshipers out of their complacency and to challenge them into surprised thought. Whether they articulated the question or not, the idea must have suggested itself somehow to their minds: which is the true worship of God? What does He want of us? Is it that we obey every detail of the ritual and sacrificial requirements as the Law of Moses insists? Or is it that we should put the greater emphasis on righteousness and mercy and ethical responsibility as the Prophet insists? In other words, the very selection of the scriptural readings forced upon the people Micah's old question, "Wherewith shall I come before the Lord and bow myself before God on high? Shall I come before Him with burnt-offerings, with calves of a year old?" To this question the prophetical reading seems to give Micah's answer (6:8), "It hath been told thee, O man, what is good and what the Lord doth require of thee: only to do justly, and to love mercy, and to walk humbly with thy God." The answer, that ethical living is almost the sole requirement (only to do justly) would be the answer left in the minds of the people if the prophetical reading stood alone in the ritual. The opposite answer, that God requires the rams and the rivers of oil for libation, in other words, the scrupulous observance of ritual, that would be the answer remaining in the minds of the people had the reading from the Torah stood alone. But it is noteworthy that the synagogue service had both of them in order that one serve as a corrective to the other and that the ultimate impression on the mind of the worshiper might be that Judaism is not Torah alone and not Prophet alone, not ritual alone and not ethics alone, neither formal observance nor mere ethicism, but ritual and ethics, pageantry and character, body and soul. This integrated, psychologically sound view of the spirit of Judaism was instilled in the hearts of the people by the very nature of the readings, so brilliantly selected.

Perhaps another illustration of the specific mood awakened in the minds of the worshipers through the very selections from Scripture is the group of readings selected from the Prophets for the weeks before and after the ninth day of the month of *Ov*. According to tradition, this day is the anniversary of the destruction of Solomon's Temple by the Babylonian armies in the sixth century before the present era and again six centuries later by the Romans in the first century of the present era. For three Sabbaths before the day of this dire double anniversary and for seven Sabbaths after it, the service includes special prophetical readings, not selected with reference to the regular weekly section from the Torah. The prophetical portions are grouped around the event of the anniversary of the destruction of the Temple. For three weeks before the ninth of *Ov*, the three prophetical readings speak of the coming destruction of the Jewish state. The first is from Jeremiah (1:14-16), in which the Prophet says: "Then the Lord said unto me: . . . For, lo, I will call all the families of the kingdoms of the north, saith the Lord; and they shall come, and they shall set every one his throne at the entrance of the gates of Jerusalem, and against all the walls thereof round about, and against all the cities of Judah. And I will utter My judgments against them touching all their wickedness; in that they have forsaken Me, and have offered unto other gods, and worshipped the work of their own hands."

The reading for the second week is from Jeremiah (2:13): "For My people have committed two evils: They have forsaken Me, the fountain of living waters, and hewed them out cisterns, broken cisterns, that can hold no water."

The third, which comes just before the anniversary of the destruction of the Temple is the great denunciatory first chapter of Isaiah, "Your new moons and your appointed seasons My soul hateth; they are a burden unto Me; I am weary to bear them. And when ye spread forth your hands, I will hide Mine eyes from you; yea, when ye make many prayers, I will not hear; your hands are full of blood. Wash you, make you clean, put away the evil of your doings from before Mine eyes . . . ; learn to do well; seek justice, relieve the oppressed, judge the fatherless, plead for the widow" (Isa. 1:14-17).

With these solemn admonitions the people enter upon the sad commemoration of the anniversary of the destruction of the Temple. Then immediately on the Sabbath following that anniversary, the first prophetical reading is the comforting courageous fortieth chapter of Isaiah: "Comfort ye, comfort ye My people, saith your God. Bid Jerusalem take heart, and proclaim unto her, that her time of service is accomplished, that her guilt is paid off; that she hath received of the Lord's hand double for all her sins" (Isa. 40:1, 2).

Then for the six following Sabbaths the prophetical readings are all from the same part of the Book of Isaiah, all enheartening, all encouraging, all comforting. The three solemn admonitions give the name to the three Sabbaths before the anniversary of the destruction. They are called the "Three of Chastisement," and the seven after the anniversary of the destruction are called "The Seven of Comforting." That very proportion is a reflection of the optimistic spirit of Judaism. While the people has suffered greatly and is aware of its unworthiness; nevertheless, its mood is not one of overwhelming dejection. On the contrary, it soon finds the spiritual resiliency to recover its courage and its hope, relying upon God's inexhaustible love. God's mercy and His forgiveness and His blessing are much greater than His anger and His condemnation and His punishment. Never are we to think of ourselves as helpless "sinners in the hands of an angry God." The mood of the synagogue service expressed by means of this group of selected readings and specifically voiced in the reading for the fifth of these Sabbaths of comforts: "For a small moment have I forsaken thee; but with great compassion will I gather thee. In a little wrath I hid My face from thee for a moment; but with everlasting kindness will I have compassion on thee, saith the Lord thy Redeemer" (Isa. 54:7, 8).

Thus the very selection of the readings inculcated in the people certain attitudes toward Judaism: a realization of its balance between ritual and ethics, of its reliance upon God's forgiveness and lovingkindness. But it also awakened in the congregation the habit of listening intently to the contrasting moods of some of the various readings and must have played an important part in their intellectual development.

Equally important was the elaborate system of translation and interpretation and study which we have discussed above. Jewish Law, Jewish life were continually changing. New laws, new enactments had come into being in order to modify and to apply the old laws to the new life. These new interpretations and new laws were derived by brilliant text analysis from the old written law of Moses and became the oral law later to be recorded in the Mishnah and Talmud. In other legal systems, such analysis and study and amplification of ancient written law to make it fit new and changing conditions, is conducted by professional jurists and discussed in the presence of technically trained lawyers. It is interesting to note that the study and the interpretation of the Law in Israel, while, of course, to a large extent conducted by trained men who devoted their lives to this particular task, was also explained and analyzed and taught in the presence of all the people whenever they gathered in the synagogue. Almost every Jew became a student of God's Law, at least one who could understand it. His intellect harmonized with the loyal impulses of his heart. Thus it was possible for the Jewish people, when later scattered all over the world, to maintain their sense of unity though many dangerous miles separated one tiny fragment of Israel from the other. All Jews trained in the synagogue to understand the Law, could fulfil it wherever they were.

Moreover, it is of special significance that this democratic education, the first that the world had ever seen, which concentrated on the study of a Law, deemed to be and revered as God's Law, was conducted as part of a synagogue service. It was part of the regular prayer-ritual. This was due to the fact that the Law was looked upon as God's Law, and the study of it no mere secular learning. It was the fulfilment of a Divine command. "And these words which I command thee this day, shall be upon thy heart; and thou shalt teach them diligently unto thy children" (Deut. 6:6).

Then, too, the effect of such study was that Judaism forever after became a religion of culture. It was natural for an ancient rabbinic book to say that without culture there can be no faith: "A boor cannot be sin-fearing nor can an ignorant man be pious" (*Ethics of the Fathers*, II, 6). Occasionally, there was a partial reaction against over-meticulous study of the minutiae of the Law, such as came with the chasidic movement of the eighteenth and nineteenth centuries. This popular movement encouraged considerable respect for the ignorant and the untutored but, in general, Judaism never revered the unlearned saint. Its saints were scholars, since the more that a man would know of the Universe the more he could appreciate the greatness of its Creator. The scholar was not a specially selected member of a learned caste; he was often a humble man, a shoemaker, a blacksmith, a burden-carrier. Scholarship was available to all and attracted all through the regular reading and interpretation of Scripture in the synagogue. All of Israel was "taught by the Lord." The very use of the synagogue service as a school for all, made God not only the great King to be adored and the Father to be loved, but the great Teacher Whose instruction we follow. "And all thy children shall be taught by the Lord; and great shall be the peace of thy children" (Isa. 54:13).

X

At Dawn I Seek Thee

EARLY MORNING PRAYERS

AT THE very beginning of the daily service
before the group of Psalms (see Chapter v) there is found a section of the
Morning Service known as the "Morning
Blessings" (Birchos Hashachar). This section is
not a formal part of the Morning Service in the
synagogue but is primarily intended for private
devotion. Its contents are somewhat difficult to
describe inasmuch as it is a combination of many
types of devotional and non-devotional material.
It contains a series of blessings which refer to
the study of the Law, also blessings which deal
with personal events of the day, selections from
the Mishnah and other rabbinic works, and also
an extra Sh'ma Yisroel to be recited very early
in the morning.

The group of small blessings (Singer *Prayerbook*, page 6 to the bottom of page 7) are prescribed in the Talmud to be recited on arising.
Thus there is a blessing to be recited at cock-

crow, another to be recited when the eyes open
("Praised be Thou . . . who openest the eyes
of the blind"), another when dressing ("Praised
be Thou . . . who clothest the naked"), another when standing upright ("Praised be Thou
. . . who raisest up them that are bowed
down"). A longer prayer follows these short
benedictions as given in the Talmud (b. B'rochos
60b) and is included in the Prayerbook with
some variations. This prayer, suitable for the
beginning of the day with its many temptations,
is given in the Talmud in the singular since it
was meant originally for private worship, but is
given in the Prayerbook in the plural now that
these prayers are printed in the public Prayerbook. This prayer reads as follows:

> May it be Thy will, O Lord our God, and God
> of our fathers, to make us familiar with Thy
> Law . . . lead us not into the power of sin or
> of temptation, keep us far from evil men and evil
> companionship, etc.

A modernized adaptation of this prayer is found
in the *Union Prayerbook*, page 102:

> May it be Thy will, O Lord our God, to lead
> us in Thy ways, that Thy name may be honored
> and Israel be blessed by our actions. May we walk
> according to the precepts of Thy law, and, re-
> maining firm in our devotion to Thee, may we
> never fall into temptation or shame. May our
> better nature always prompt us to discharge our

duties faithfully and to do good with a willing heart. Gird us with strength to govern our inclinations in accordance with Thy will. Grant, O Father, that by our conduct we may win favor in Thine eyes and in the eyes of our fellowmen.

Among these various early morning prayers and sections for study and blessings, are two which merit especial discussion: one, the prayer taken from the Talmud (*ibid.*), "Lord the soul which Thou hast given me is pure"; and the other, likewise from the Talmud (b. Yomo 87b), "Lord of all worlds." The first of these two prayers as given in the Talmud and quoted in the Prayerbook reads as follows (Singer *Prayerbook*, page 5):

> O my God, the soul which thou gavest me is pure; thou didst create it, thou didst form it, thou didst breathe it into me; thou preservest it within me; and thou wilt take it from me, but wilt restore it unto me hereafter. So long as the soul is within me, I will give thanks unto thee, O Lord my God and God of my fathers, Sovereign of all works, Lord of all souls! Blessed art thou, O Lord, who restorest souls unto dead bodies.

The prayer clearly refers to the time of awakening from sleep, for which time of day it is provided in the Talmud. It is based upon the idea that the soul leaves the body during sleep and that God restores the soul to the body on awakening. Hence, too, the phrase in the hymn "*Adon Olom*," based upon Psalm 31:6, "In His hand

I put my spirit when asleep and when awake."
This also explains the "seal" of the prayer on
awakening in the morning, "Praised be Thou
Who restorest the soul to dead bodies." In the
body of the prayer this idea is, of course, connected with death and resurrection.

The most significant idea in the prayer is found
in the opening sentence, "Lord, the soul which
Thou hast given to me is pure." Judaism never
believed in the doctrine of original sin in the
sense that the soul of man, because of the sin of
Adam, is forever tainted and cannot be redeemed
from its inherited corruption except by special
grace. True, the rabbis were psychologists
enough to know and to refer frequently to the
Yetser Ho-ro, the "evil inclination," in man
which tempts him to sin, and, indeed, they make
passing reference to the "poison of the snake,"
the sin caused by the disobedience of Eve at the
temptation of the serpent. But this evil inclination is balanced by the *Yetser Ha-tov*, the "good
inclination," and, furthermore, man through
prayer and good deeds can overcome the evil inclination within him. But the soul itself as received by man is not corrupt. It is within man's
power to keep it pure. The rabbis commented
(b. Shabos 152b) on the verse in Ecclesiastes
(12:7), "And the dust returneth to the earth as
it was, and the spirit returneth unto God Who

gave it," and said that as God gave us the spirit pure so we should return it to Him pure. Thus morning after morning, either at home or in the synagogue, the Jew recites this grand assertion, "Lord, the soul which Thou hast given me is pure." (See Kohler, *Jewish Theology*, Chapter xxxv, and Schechter, *Some Aspects of Rabbinic Theology*, Chapter xv ff.) As a matter of fact, there is a tendency in Judaism to believe in the very converse of the doctrine of original sin, namely, the doctrine of the merit of the fathers. The rabbis of the Talmud believed that the nobility of the patriarchs descended as a blessing to their children. In other words, instead of inherited sin they believed in a sort of inherited virtue. (Compare Schechter, *Some Aspects of Rabbinic Theology*, Chapter xii.) Of this famous prayer in the early Morning Service, the *Union Prayerbook* has the following version:

The soul which Thou, O God, hast given unto me came pure from Thee. Thou hast created it, Thou hast formed it, Thou hast breathed it into me; Thou hast preserved it in this body and, at the appointed time, Thou wilt take it from this earth that it may enter upon life everlasting. While the breath of life is within me, I will worship Thee, Sovereign of the world and Lord of all souls. Praised be Thou, O God, in Whose hands are the souls of all the living and the spirits of all flesh.

The second prayer, "Lord of all worlds," is connected in thought with the one just discussed. (Singer *Prayerbook*, bottom of page 8; *Union Prayerbook*, page 101: "Lord of all worlds, etc.") This prayer, referred to in the Talmud (b. Yomo 87b), was part of the confessional service of the Day of Atonement, as its thought and penitential moods clearly indicate.

> Lord of all worlds, not in reliance upon our own merit do we lay our supplications before Thee, but trusting in Thine infinite mercy alone. For what are we, what is our life, what our goodness, what our power? What can we say in Thy presence? Are not all the mighty men as naught before Thee and those of great renown as though they had never been; the wisest as if without knowledge, and men of understanding as if without discernment? Many of our works are vain, and our days pass away like a shadow. Our life would be altogether vanity, were it not for the soul which, fashioned in Thine own image, gives us assurance of our higher destiny and imparts to our fleeting days an abiding value. (*Union Prayerbook*, page 101.)

The thought of this prayer is clear enough, namely, that although it is incumbent upon us to keep our soul righteous and pure by our actions and by obedience to God's commandments, yet we know that we fall short of the goal which God sets for us. "For there is not a righteous man upon earth, that doeth good, and sinneth not" (Eccles. 7:20). We depend upon God's aid not

· 117 ·

only to help us overcome our evil inclinations but we must come to God for forgiveness for all the evil which we have done. Hence, not relying upon the righteousness in us, but upon God's abundant mercy do we offer our supplications to Him. In the Orthodox Prayerbook, this prayer continues with a reference to the merit of the patriarchs, which we hope will sustain us. (Singer *Prayerbook*, page 9: "Nevertheless we are thy people . . . the children of Abraham, thy friend . . . the seed of Isaac, his only son, who was bound upon the altar, etc.")

These prayers, whether recited at home as originally intended, or privately in the synagogue before the public worship begins, form a fitting introduction to the devotions of the day. They assert man's essential goodness but they are aware of man's weakness. They ask humbly for God's forgiveness. Confidently turning towards God for aid, man offers his supplication at the beginning of the day.

Our discussion so far (beginning with Chapter v), dealt with the daily Morning Service in the synagogue. In succeeding chapters we shall discuss other services of the synagogue year. It will be observed that the liturgical structure of all the other services have a definite relationship to the daily Morning Service with which we have dealt in detail. The elements of this service are basic to all the rest. The various Holiday Services, the Sabbath Service, are all elaborations or variations from elements found in the daily Morning Service.

The daily Afternoon and Evening Services, likewise, can easily be understood on the basis of the analysis of the Morning Service. They do not require any elaborate description.

Daily Afternoon Service. The Afternoon Service is understood to correspond to the regular afternoon sacrifice (the Tomid) in the Temple on Mount Zion. Since the nineteen-blessing group of petitional prayers (the T'filo) is supposed to be the Prayerbook equivalent of the regular sacrifice (cf. Chapter VII), the essential element in the Afternoon Service is the T'filo. This is preceded by Psalm 145. The rabbis consider this Psalm a particularly beautiful one and appropriate for prayer, perhaps because of verse 16: "Thou openest Thy hand, and satisfiest every living thing with Thy favor." They recommend that this Psalm be recited three times a day (b. B'rochos 4b). It is recited twice during the Morning Service and this recitation before the T'filo of the Afternoon Service makes the third time. After the Psalm there follows the T'filo, which is the essential part of the service; then the service concludes as do all services with the Adoration (Olenu) (cf. Chapter XIV).

Daily Evening Service. There was no sacrifice at night in the Temple, therefore, in the night prayer there is properly speaking no public T'filo, which corresponds to the regular sacrifice. Hence, the T'filo in the Evening Service is recited silently and not repeated for the congregation by the cantor. The essential part of the Evening Service is not the T'filo but the Sh'ma with its blessings. Inasmuch as the Sh'ma Yisroel is to be recited "when thou liest down and when thou risest up," the Morning Service and the Evening Service are built around the Sh'ma. The two blessings before the Sh'ma in the Morning Services are repeated in idea though with simpler language in the Evening Service: the first blessing expressing the thought of God, the Lord of nature; and the second, God the Master and Teacher in history. Then follows as in the morning, Sh'ma Yisroel, "And thou shalt love the Lord thy God." After the Sh'ma comes, as in the morning, the blessing of redemption, mentioning the first great redemption, the Exodus from Egypt (see Chapter VI).

The difference between the Sh'ma and its blessings in the evening from the Sh'ma and its blessings in the morning is first, as we have said, that the ideas expressed in the blessings are in simpler language in the evening; and secondly, that after the Sh'ma instead of there being one blessing as in the morning (the blessing of redemption) there are two blessings. This second blessing, found only in the Evening Service, is essentially a night prayer. It begins, "Cause us, O Lord our God, to lie down in peace." (Singer *Prayerbook*, page 135, bottom to the middle of page 136; *Union Prayerbook*, page 5.) After this comes the T'filo, which is not repeated by the cantor, then follows the Adoration (Olenu), which concludes every service.

XI

Gift of New Soul

THE SABBATH SERVICE

O F ALL the services in the synagogue the Sabbath Service must have exerted the deepest influence on the life of the wor- shipers. On the Sabbath the whole community gathered for study and worship. During the week of work, attendance at the synagogue was small; men generally read the daily services at home; teachers and students often prayed in the school- house or at their studies. The daily services, of course, exercised a constant spiritual influence but they lacked the inspiring presence of an entire community assembled for worship.

On Mondays and Thursdays, the market days, there were larger gatherings in the synagogue since on these days people came to the cities for trade. These two days were established as court days. The synagogue services were more fully attended, and, therefore, the services were more elaborate. More prayer material was added, par- ticularly in later times (see Chapter VIII), and a supplementary reading of Scripture became customary (see Chapter IX). But on the Sabbath, when all work ceased, the whole community gathered in the synagogue and the services were beautified. The complete weekly portion from Scripture was read as well as the traditional selection from the Prophets. Of course, the services for the great festivals, Passover, Shovuos, and Sukos, were still more elaborate, and the services for the High Holidays, the New Year and the Day of Atonement, were profoundly impressive. But these occasions came but once a year whereas the influence of the Sabbath was repeated week after week.

The Sabbath was unique as an institution and was recognized as unique as soon as the Jews came in contact with the Greco-Roman world. We who are so accustomed to the idea of resting one day a week almost feel that it is inherent in nature and can hardly realize what life would be like if the days went on in an unbroken succession with no regular grouping or division for variety and rest. But thus, indeed, it was in the western world before the Jewish influence, directly through Judaism and later through the daughter-religion, Christianity, made itself felt. In Rome those who owned slaves never worked, and those who were slaves never rested. The idea that all human beings (and according to the

Bible even beasts of burden) have the right and the duty to rest one day in seven was a new and startling idea. The observance of the Jewish day of rest began to spread rapidly in Rome. But Roman writers said many bitter things about it. They spoke of it as a waste of one-seventh of one's entire life. They sneered at the growing demand of slaves for a rest every seventh day; but the Sabbath could not be laughed away. Once it was made known to the world it was bound to be accepted for it was based upon the right of man as a child of God Who rested on the seventh day of the Creation of the world. The humane institution of the Sabbath thus left its permanent mark upon civilization.

Like all the great and creative ideas found in Judaism this Sabbath idea also had its contact with earlier and more primitive customs. Among primitive tribes there were certain days throughout the year when it was considered wrong or taboo to work. They were unlucky days. In ancient Babylonian civilization these unlucky days, days of ill-omen, occurred with a degree of regularity since they were connected with the phases of the moon. Perhaps the first day marked by the Babylonians as unlucky, was the fifteenth of the month when the moon became full and seemed for a moment to rest from its changes. This developed into the custom of marking the four phases of the moon, the seventh, the four-teenth, the twenty-first, and the twenty-eighth days of the month. Of course, since the Baby-lonian month varied from twenty-nine to thirty days, the last week of the month had eight or nine days; but on these fairly regular occasions a Sabbath was ordained. The mood of this Sab-bath was equivalent to the mood of the occasional rest-days of still more primitive times. They were taboo days on which it was danger-ous or unlucky to begin any enterprise. Of this primitive material the Jewish Sabbath was built.

The Bible reveals, unmistakably, in its ordinance for the Sabbath a decided change from all these older ideas. In the first place, the Sabbath was freed from any connection with the phases of the moon. It took place regularly every seventh day, thus breaking any superstitious connection with the moon. It was connected instead with God's work in creation. God completed His work at the end of the sixth day and we in emulation of God, likewise rest on the seventh. The seventh day became a day of covenant between God and man and was meant to be an evidence to man of the presence in the world of God the Creator. Thus (Ezek. 20:20), "And hallow My Sabbaths, and they shall be a sign between Me and you, that ye may know that I am the Lord your God." It was a covenant, a bond between God the Creator and man the worker. "Six days shall work be done, but on the seventh day is a Sabbath of solemn rest, holy to the Lord; . . . wherefore the children of Israel shall keep the Sabbath, . . . it is a sign between Me and the children of Israel forever; for in six days the Lord made heaven and earth, and on the seventh day He ceased from work and rested" (Exod. 31:15-17). The biblical concept of the Sabbath as a mark of comradeship between man and God in their work in the world is an immense advance over the superstitious day of ill-omen connected with the phases of the moon found in earlier religions.

But a still further development and deepening of the idea of the Sabbath is found chiefly in the Prayerbook. The Bible emphasized the Sabbath as a day on which work is forbidden because the day is a bond between Israel and God. But the Prayerbook adds so many spiritual ideas that it would be impossible to explain the profound influence of the Sabbath on the life of Israel without them. A study of the ritual for the Sabbath day will show how the idea of the Sabbath was deepened in the Prayerbook and the Synagogue.

The Sabbath and also, of course, the Sabbath Service, begin at sunset Friday night. In the Jewish calendar the day begins at sunset and ends the following sunset. The scriptural basis for this custom is generally taken from the story of Creation where the days are marked as beginning in the evening and ending the following evening (cf. Chapter xx). Thus the first Sabbath Service is on Friday night and the service on Saturday night at the outgoing of the Sabbath is no longer a Sabbath Service but a Week-day Service, actually, the first service of Sunday.

There are four services on the Sabbath: the Sabbath Eve Service on Friday night (Kabolas Shabos, "The Reception of the Sabbath"); the Sabbath Morning Service and the Sabbath Afternoon Service; and since the services were supposed to correspond to the regular offerings in the Temple and there was on the Sabbath day an additional Sabbath offering, there is an additional service for the Sabbath (Musof). This additional service is combined with the Morning Service but is technically a fourth service. The Reform Prayerbook omits the Musof on Sabbath and on holidays.

A. Friday Evening. The opening service of the Sabbath on Friday evening, the Reception of the Sabbath, being an Evening Service, consists just as all Evening Services primarily of the Sh'ma and its accompanying benedictions (see Chapter vi). However, before the Sh'ma and its blessings open the service with the usual invocation, *"Bor'chu es adonoy,"* "Praise ye the Lord

Who is to be praised," certain psalms have come to be used. Originally only Psalms 92 and 93 were recited. These psalms, of course, belong to the Friday Evening Service, and are mentioned in the Mishnah as the psalms recited by the Levites: 92 for Sabbath and 93 for Friday. In the sixteenth century the Cabalistic movement, which centered in the city of Safed, in Palestine, and was fostered largely by exiles and the descendants of exiles from Spain, added a number of psalms to be recited at the Reception of the Sabbath. To express the idea of Sabbath joy, the Sabbath was looked upon as a bride who was to be greeted happily. This idea has a talmudic basis (b. Sabbath 119a). The Cabalist groups in Safed would put on white garments and go forth in joy to meet the Sabbath bride. On their march they would sing psalms for joy: Psalm 95, "O come, let us sing unto the Lord; let us shout for joy to the Rock of our salvation"; Psalm 96, "O sing unto the Lord a new song, etc.," to Psalm 99. These psalms were made thereafter a regular part of the service of the Reception of the Sabbath. One of the Safed group, the poet, Solomon al kabetz Halevi, also wrote a hymn welcoming the Sabbath bride. This hymn *L'cho Dodi*: "O come my friend to meet the bride, let us welcome the presence of the Sabbath," likewise became a regular part of the Reception of the Sabbath in all rituals. (Singer *Prayerbook*, pp. 155 ff.; *Union Prayerbook*, pp. 8 ff., also the Hymn: "Beloved, come, the bride to meet," page 26.)

While the custom of reciting these psalms and singing the hymn of Solomon al kabetz Halevi goes back no earlier than the sixteenth century, yet it was adopted by almost all Jewish communities since it expressed completely the traditional spirit of the Sabbath as it developed in the Jewish service. The Sabbath, with its strict prohibition of work and of kindling fire and light, could easily have become a day of gloom and dread, a day of ill-omen, as, indeed, it was among the Babylonians. But from the very beginning the effort was made to express the joy inherent in the day of rest, an evidence of man's happy kinship with God, the Creator. The late passage in Isaiah (58:13) already adds the concept of the joy of the Sabbath to the older concept of refraining from work. It reads, "If thou turn away thy foot because of the Sabbath, from pursuing thy business on My holy day; and call the Sabbath a delight, and the holy of the Lord honourable; and shalt honour it, not doing thy wonted ways, nor pursuing thy business, nor speaking thereof; then shalt thou delight thyself in the Lord."

The Talmud, likewise, is careful to devise legislation to intensify the joy of the Sabbath and to guard it from degenerating into a day of gloom. It recommends better clothes, finer food, refraining from fasting or sorrow. This mood of happiness finds its fullest expression in the Sabbath Service, in the joyous hymns taken from the Psalms which precede the Reception of the Sabbath, in the wording of all prayers and even in the happy table hymns at the Sabbath meal.

After the Sh'ma and its benedictions which follow the opening Psalm, comes the T'filo, the petitional prayer, for the Sabbath. Since the T'filo is understood to correspond to the regular offering at the Temple, and since there was no regular offering at the Temple at night, this evening T'filo, like the T'filo in all Evening Services, is not repeated aloud by the reader or cantor (see Chapter VII).

The T'filo on Friday like all the T'filos on the Sabbath has the same three introductory benedictions, "the Patriarchs," "God's Might," "God's Holiness," and the three concluding benedictions used in every T'filo: that God will receive our prayers, our thanks for His providence, and the prayer for peace. But the thirteen intervening prayers used every day to voice the petitions of daily life during the week of work, have no place on the Sabbath. Instead of these thirteen intervening prayers, the Sabbath has only one intervening prayer which deals with the theme of the Sabbath. (Singer *Prayerbook*, page 166 to page 171, from "Blessed art thou, O Lord our God and God of our fathers, God of Abraham, etc.," to "Blessed art thou, O Lord, who blessest thy people Israel with peace." For the one intervening prayer in place of the thirteen of every day, page 168, "Thou didst hallow the seventh day," up to top of page 169, "Blessed art thou, O Lord, who hallowest the Sabbath." *Union Prayerbook*, the T'filo of Friday evening, page 18, "Praised be Thou, O Lord, God of our fathers, God of Abraham, etc.," to bottom of page 22, "Praised be Thou, O Lord, Giver of peace." For the one intervening prayer, from page 20, "Heavenly Father, we rejoice," to the middle of page 22, "Praised be Thou O Lord, Who sanctifiest the Sabbath.")

After the T'filo, the wine ceremony ushering in the Sabbath, the Kiddush, is recited. The Kiddush, primarily a home ceremony, is recited in the synagogue on Friday night for the benefit of strangers, who in former times were frequently housed in the synagogue. (Singer *Prayerbook*, pp. 176, 181; *Union Prayerbook*, page 93.)

B. Morning Service. The Morning Service for the Sabbath is identical in construction with the regular Morning Service. It includes the chapters of Psalms, then the Sh'ma and its blessings, then the T'filo, then the reading of the Torah (see Chapter IX). This system of prayer, the same as that of every day, is, however, amplified for the Sabbath. In the chapters of Psalms before the Sh'ma, additional Psalms and other prayers are inserted, as for example, Psalm 19, "The heavens declare the glory of God," Psalm 90 and Psalm 91, Psalm 33 (see Singer *Prayerbook*, pp. 26-28, also page 30). The Yotser, the section of the Sh'ma and its blessings, is also somewhat amplified. The T'filo for Sabbath morning, like the T'filo for all Sabbaths and festivals, has seven benedictions, that is, one special benediction in place of the thirteen intervening petitions for every day. (Singer *Prayerbook*, page 197 to page 206, and for the one intervening blessing, the bottom of page 200 to page 201, "Blessed art thou, O Lord, who hallowest the Sabbath"; *Union Prayerbook*, pp. 124-141, and the various forms of the intervening blessing from pp. 128-138: "Praised be Thou, O Lord, Who sanctifiest the Sabbath.") After the T'filo comes the regular weekly reading of the Torah, the full weekly portion, and the regular prophetic portion, as described in Chapter IX. Following the reading of the Torah there are prayers for the welfare of those who support the Law and the congregation and also for the government. (Singer *Prayerbook* from page 217, "May salvation from heaven, etc.," to the bottom of page 219: "O that this may be his will, and let us say, Amen." *Union Prayerbook*, page 147 bottom: "Thou, Who art the source of all blessings," down to page 148: "exalt our nation in righteousness. Amen.")

Then in Orthodox Services (and generally in the Conservative Services) comes the additional (Musof) T'filo, also a seven-blessing T'filo, corresponding to the additional Sabbath sacrifice in the Temple (Singer *Prayerbook*, pp. 226-237). The concluding prayers, Olenu (the Adoration) (Singer *Prayerbook*, page 240; *Union Prayerbook*, page 150), and the Kaddish (Singer *Prayerbook*, page 242; *Union Prayerbook*, page 152) will be discussed in Chapter XIV.

C. *Afternoon Service*. Since the Sh'ma is to be recited at sunrise and sunset ("when thou liest down and when thou risest up"), there is no Sh'ma in the Afternoon Service (see Chapter VI). But since there was an afternoon sacrifice in the Temple, the Afternoon Service consists of the T'filo, the petitional prayer, which is understood to correspond with the regular sacrifice. This is a seven-blessing T'filo as in all Sabbath Services (Singer *Prayerbook*, pp. 254-260; *Union Prayerbook*, page 162). On Sabbath afternoon also, the Torah is taken out but the reading then consists only of the first portion for the following Sabbath, which is also read the next Monday morning and the next Thursday morning. After the T'filo certain psalms (Psalms 104; 120-134) are read in the winter months on Sabbath afternoon and in the summer months a chapter of the *Ethics of the Fathers*. (Singer *Prayerbook*, page 271, bottom, ff.; *Union Prayerbook*, page 163 ff.)

This concludes the Sabbath Service except that the Saturday Evening Service (which really is the first service for Sunday) has a special prayer marking the outgoing of the Sabbath and a special wine service corresponding to the Kiddush, which ushered in the Sabbath. This wine service concluding the Sabbath, is called *Havdolo*, and speaks of the distinctions between the sacred and profane, Sabbath and week-day (Singer *Prayerbook*, page 310).

The entire Sabbath day exerted its influence upon the worshiper. Most of the day was spent in the synagogue. The Evening Service of the Reception of the Sabbath was longer than the week-day Evening Services. The Morning Service was more elaborate than the week-day Morning Services. And after the Afternoon Service, the men usually remained to study and to listen to learned discourses. As the day began on Friday evening and then slowly waned Saturday afternoon, the mood of the Sabbath changed and different ideas, suitable to the passing hours, were expressed.

Although the three main T'filos of the Sabbath, the Evening, the Morning, and the Afternoon, were all seven-blessing T'filos, yet each differed from the other, and it would be interesting to notice their different moods. On Friday evening, the intervening blessing of the T'filo reads substantially as follows, "Thou didst hallow the seventh day unto Thy Name as the end of the creation of heaven and earth . . . and the heaven and earth were finished and all their hosts." The Sabbath morning T'filo has as its intervening prayer-thought the following, "Moses rejoiced in the gift of his portion, a diadem of glory didst Thou place on his head on Mount Sinai when he brought the two tables of stone on which the observance of the Sabbath was prescribed: 'and the children of Israel shall keep the Sabbath, etc.' " In the Afternoon Service the intervening blessing reads as follows, "Thou art One and Thy Name is One; who is like unto Thy people Israel, a unique nation on earth."

It is to be noticed that these three T'filos, Friday evening, Sabbath morning, and Sabbath afternoon, taken in succession as the day went by, expressed almost the same succession of thought found in the great climax of the daily service, the Yotser, that is, the Sh'ma and its accompanying blessings. As the first blessing before the Sh'ma began with a great description of God in nature Who brings the light and creates the world, so does the first T'filo blessing for the Sabbath, recited on Friday evening, speak of the God of nature Who gave the Sabbath when He created the world and rested from His work. As the second blessing before the Sh'ma every day is the blessing of the Law and speaks of God as the Guide in history and our Teacher of His Law, so does the second T'filo of the Sabbath speak of the giving of the Law to Moses on Mount Sinai, who rejoiced to receive it and to give the observance of the Sabbath to the people of Israel as their teacher and guide. And just as in the daily service, the two concepts of God, God as Creator and God as Teacher, are merged in the great sentence, "Hear O Israel, the Lord our God, the Lord is One," so does the third T'filo of the Sabbath, in the Afternoon Service, merge the two thoughts and say, "Thou art One and Thy Name is One." Indeed, the parallel is still closer. As the Sh'ma Yisroel continues with the remainder of the quotation from Deuteronomy in which parents are enjoined: "And these words which I command Thee . . . Thou shalt teach them diligently unto thy children," so the Sabbath afternoon declaration of God's unity speaks of Abraham rejoicing and Isaac being glad and Jacob and his children resting thereon, and ends, "Let thy children perceive and know that this their rest is from Thee and by their rest may they hallow Thy Name." The *Union Prayerbook* extends this thought in its version of the Sabbath Afternoon Service, page 162, "Heavenly Father, Thou art One, and Thy Name is One; may Thy truth unite all mankind unto one holy bond of brotherhood, and may our love for one another be our crown of glory and armor of strength. Bless us, O God, on this Sabbath, and grant that it be unto us a day of perfect rest and sanctification."

This parallel of the successive ideas in the sequence of these prayers for the Sabbath, with the sequence of ideas in the blessings and paragraphs of the daily Sh'ma, is too close to be accidental. It might not have been consciously achieved; if so it is all the more remarkable an evidence of the unconscious hold that this sequence of ideas had on Jewry and on its Prayerbook. As every day we think of God as Creator, Teacher, and our Beloved Friend, so we think, too, of the Sabbath and its rest and joy as a covenant with the Creator, with the Teacher, and with the only One to Whom our soul turns in love.

This spiritual and intimate mood of the Sabbath has rarely been appreciated by non-Jewish scholars. In fact, the New Testament itself misunderstands the Sabbath. The Gospel (Matt. 17;

Mark 2; Luke 6) reports that Jesus disputed with the Pharisees with regard to the Sabbath day. He violated the Sabbath laws against work and argued from biblical precedent to justify this violation and then said, "The Sabbath was made for man and not man for the Sabbath." That statement of Jesus is not contrary to the rabbinic law and its spirit as the writer of the Gospel implies. It is always understood in Jewish Law that the Sabbath may be broken in an emergency, such as saving a life, curing the sick, and so forth. In fact, the very statement that the Sabbath was given to man to break when necessary is itself found in rabbinic sources (see Schechter, *Some Aspects of Rabbinic Theology*, page 152, M'chilto to Exod. 31:13). The writer of the Gospel misunderstood the whole spirit of the Sabbath as it developed in Jewish thought and as it was manifest particularly in the Prayerbook. Following the lead of the Gospel, other non-Jewish writers even up to modern times, depicted the Sabbath as a day of dread and gloom in which man was hemmed in by multitudinous restrictions and was unable to do anything but sit motionless in his home. It was this gloomy picture of the Jewish Sabbath derived ultimately from the New Testament's misunderstanding which led to the stern and harsh Sunday observance of Puritan times. The student of Jewish life, particularly of the Jewish services in the synagogue and home, knows that this picture is entirely distorted. All the multitudinous Jewish laws guarding against Sabbath violations, were not a burden in a Jewish environment in the days when they were ordained. When an entire society does no business and no work on a certain day there is very little need or desire for any individual to be an exception. The laws reflected the normal mode of life. It was no hardship to obey them. But aside from this obvious fact, the mood of the Sabbath Service was one of joy. The fathers of the synagogue selected the happy psalms for the Sabbath. They spoke of the delight of the Sabbath. All the later songs produced by subsequent generations inspired by the ritual of the Sabbath day, were poems of joy and of happiness. A festival which created hymns of joy for centuries could hardly have been a gloomy day, hemmed in by the wall of countless restrictions, as the Sabbath was misunderstood to have been.

The fact of the matter is, the Sabbath of the synagogue and the home, the Sabbath as it developed under the influence of the Jewish prayer ritual, created an entirely new understanding of rest from work. The old superstitious idea that it was unlucky to work on this day, was converted into a positive concept of rest. Then the idea of rest was enriched in a profoundly spiritual way. Rest became not merely a negative refraining from work but a positive recreation of the soul. In the first place it was rest from hard labor, hence, all the various laws to keep the people from any sort of work. Then it became rest of the spirit from grief and worry. Hence, fasting was prohibited on this day; worrying was prohibited on this day. Even when the sick were visited on the Sabbath the visitor said: it is Sabbath, it is forbidden to worry, God will send healing. Daily cares, as well as daily tasks, were set aside and out of repose of the spirit came the joy of the spirit, thus the Sabbath became a day of happiness.

In another sense, also, the Sabbath became a day of rest. It took the mind away from daily cares and daily business and positively turned one's thoughts in a new direction. This was the day of the study of God's Law. The people in the synagogue heard the Law read and interpreted; during the afternoon they often heard special discourses or studied the *Ethics of the Fathers*. Their mind was immersed in eternal things, a spirit different from the week-day spirit rose in them. No wonder they expressed it in pictorial terms when they said that an extra soul came to every child of Israel on the Sabbath. Hence, the Sabbath brought with it a new radiance and a new beauty every week. How natural it was for the day to be greeted by the rabbis in the Talmud; one of whom put on beautiful garments and said, "I am going forth to greet the Sabbath Queen." And another, beautifully arrayed, said in greeting, "Come O (Sabbath) Bride" (b. Sabbath 119a).

Whether they thought of the Sabbath as the remembrance of God's completed work at Creation or of God who taught them His Law on this day, the rabbis gave the word "rest" not a negative but a positive connotation, a day of the rebuilding of the spirit, a day of radiant spiritual peace. This mood of radiant peace breathes through all the Sabbath prayers and is beautifully expressed in the closing paragraph of the intervening prayer in every Sabbath T'filo. "Our God and God of our fathers, accept our rest; sanctify us by thy commandments and grant our portion in thy Law, satisfy us with thy goodness, and gladden us with thy salvation; purify our hearts to serve thee in truth; and in thy love and favor, O Lord our God, let us inherit thy holy Sabbath; and may Israel, who hallow thy name, rest thereon. Blessed art thou, O Lord, who hallowest the Sabbath" (Singer *Prayerbook*, page 201). The version in the *Union Prayerbook*, page 22, is as follows: "Our God and God of our fathers, grant that our worship on this

Sabbath be acceptable to Thee. Sanctify us through Thy commandments that we may share in the blessings of Thy word. Teach us to be satisfied with the gifts of Thy goodness and gratefully to rejoice in all Thy mercies. Purify our hearts that we may serve Thee in truth. O help us to preserve the Sabbath as Israel's heritage from generation to generation, that it may ever bring rest and joy, peace and comfort to the dwellings of our brethren, and through it Thy name be hallowed in all the earth. Praised be Thou, O Lord, Who sanctifiest the Sabbath."

If one would read merely a list of the legal minutiae of the strict Sabbath laws, he might come to the mistaken conclusion to which some writers have come, that the Sabbath was a burden and an enslavement to Israel. But if he knew the spirit of many of the non-legal expressions of the rabbis and through them understood the motive of the laws, his opinion would be corrected; but particularly if he would read the text and absorb the spirit of the Prayerbook, he would discover that the Sabbath was not a day of enforced idleness but a day of radiant peace.

The whole mood of the Sabbath rest is expressed in the fourth prayer of the T'filo of the Sabbath Afternoon Service (Singer *Prayerbook*, page 256):

Abraham was glad, Isaac rejoiced, Jacob and

his sons rested thereon:—a rest vouchsafed in generous love, a true and faithful rest, a rest in peace and tranquillity, in quietude and safety, a perfect rest wherein thou delightest. Let thy children perceive and know that this their rest is from thee, and by their rest may they hallow thy name.

XII

Thou Shalt Rejoice

THE FESTIVAL SERVICE

THE three festivals, Passover, Shovuos and Sukos, are the most ancient holidays in Israel. They are the outcome of a long and complex historical development. A great deal of scholarship has been applied towards discovering their origin. Some of them, specifically the Passover, evidently had originally a primitive pastoral form, going back to the time when the Israelites were shepherds and lived in the desert. Later, the festivals showed traces of an agricultural celebration, following the phases of the harvest. These clearly go back to the time when the Israelites were settled agriculturists in the land of Palestine. Furthermore, all of them have historical implications, each being connected with some great event in the history of the past.

All these strands of origin are woven together by the time the festivals appear as part of the Prayerbook ritual. And while the origins are of importance for technical scholarship, they played no part in the influence of the festivals upon the life of the Jewish people after the Prayerbook arose. In the Prayerbook the festivals already bespeak a definite idea, combined, indeed, of many original sources but now a harmonized unity.

The agricultural basis of the three festivals was much clearer in the celebration of the festivals in the great Temple at Jerusalem than it was in the various synagogues scattered through the land. In the first place, these three festivals were known as Pilgrim Festivals (*R'golim*). The Bible already required that at these three times during the year every male in Israel appear at the Temple to celebrate the festival in Jerusalem. (Exod. 23:14): "Three times thou shalt keep a feast unto Me in the year"; verse 17, "Three times in the year all thy males shall appear before the Lord God." These three periods, when the three festivals were celebrated by pilgrimages, came at significant periods in the agricultural year. Passover came at the close of the winter and the beginning of the spring when the very earliest grain (the barley) ripened. The seven weeks between Passover and Shovuos marked the ripening of all the other grains in succession. Shovuos marked, therefore, the end of the grain harvest and the beginning of the fruit harvest. Hence it, too, was a dividing mark in the agricultural year and the beginning of the period of bringing of the first-fruits to Jerusalem. Thus, it was a natural time for a pilgrimage. The four months from Shovuos to Sukos was the time when the various fruits ripened in succession. Sukos, therefore, represented the end of all the harvests. This, too, was a natural time for a pilgrimage to Jerusalem. At these three periods of the year, Jerusalem was jammed to overflowing with pilgrims who came to celebrate the holidays in the presence of the Lord at the Temple.

The harvest season, beginning in the spring and ending in the autumn, was marked at its opening and its close with especially elaborate ceremonies in the Temple. The beginning of the harvest season, Passover, was marked with a special ritual in the Temple on the first day of the feast. A procession from the Temple went down to a previously selected barley field. A sheaf of barley was taken and at once winnowed and milled, and made into a meal-offering amid great solemnity. After that ceremony the people of Jerusalem were permitted to eat of the newly harvested grain. Thus was the new year's harvest inaugurated.

The festival of Sukos, which marked the close of the entire harvest period, also had an elaborate ceremonial to signalize it in the Temple at Jerusalem. The harvest now was ended and the winter was beginning. Winter in Palestine is the rainy season and rain is essential for the growing of the crops. Hence, water ceremonies or rain ceremonies formed an important part of the Sukos celebration in the Temple. At the Morning Service of each of the days of Sukos a water libation was offered together with the pouring out of the wine at the altar. In addition to this daily water libation, there was an elaborate festival of the "Drawing of the Water" on the first night of Sukos. The Temple courts were illuminated and a great celebration with dancing and song took place. It is evident that the agricultural nature of the three pilgrim festivals had their finest and fullest expression in the Temple which was the natural focus of the harvest celebration.

These harvest celebrations in the Temple had their effect upon the various synagogues scattered throughout the land and left their mark upon the synagogue service and the Prayerbook. Of course, great elaborate folk festivals celebrated in the Temple could hardly be celebrated in the synagogue but some evidence of the agricultural year is easily discernible. Reminiscent of the solemn bringing of the first barley sheaf on the Passover to the Temple was the fact that at the end of the first day of Passover, the day when the *Omer* (measure) of barley was waved in the Temple, the synagogue service provided that the day be declared the first day of the *Omer* of the "waving." The next day is called the second day of the *Omer*, and, thereafter, the *Omer* is counted in the synagogue for forty-nine days, until at the end of forty-nine days the Feast of Weeks, Shovuos, is celebrated. Perhaps also the fact that Passover is a spring harvest festival explains why the Song of Songs was selected to be read on Passover. This Book breathes the mood of springtime, "For, lo, the winter is past, the rain is over and gone; the flowers appear on the earth, the time of singing is come, and the voice of the turtle is heard in our land" (Song of Songs 2:11, 12). Furthermore, since the winter is over and the rains of winter past, the farmer needs the heavy dew of Palestine to help ripen the crops. Hence, the synagogue service for the first day of Passover includes a prayer for dew, T'filas Tal (*Union Prayerbook*, page 265).

Shovuos, in the synagogue service, shows no especial evidence of the influence of the Palestinian agricultural life. However, Sukos clearly recalls old agricultural memories. It is the close of the harvest. The people dwell in harvest booths; they wave the *lulov* and the *esrog*, the fruits required to be waved at this harvest festival. "Howbeit on the fifteenth day of the seventh month, when ye have gathered in the fruits of the land, ye shall keep the feast of the Lord seven days; on the first day shall be a solemn rest, and on the eighth day shall be a solemn rest. And ye shall take you on the first day the fruit of goodly trees, branches of palm-trees, and boughs of thick trees, and willows of the brook, and ye shall rejoice before the Lord your God seven days" (Lev. 23:39, 40). Also, there is a reminiscence of the water celebration of Temple times in that on the last day of Sukos in the synagogue service, there is a special prayer for rain, T'filas Geshem, in the *Union Prayerbook*, page 265.

While the synagogue service had these evidences of the agricultural elements in the three festivals, the greater emphasis was not agricultural but historical. Each one of these festivals was thought to be based upon some historic event in the history of Israel. In the intervening prayer of the holiday T'filo as well as in the Kiddush wine service, all three festivals are described as a "memorial of the going out from Egypt." The three specific historical events based upon biblical narrative are each a part of the larger event of the Exodus. Thus, Passover dealt with the deliverance from Egypt itself and is always referred to in the T'filo as "the time of our freedom." Shovuos is connected with the giving of the Law on Mount Sinai and is thus referred to as "the time of the giving of our Law." It was difficult to find a historic incident in the story of the Exodus in the desert to fit the feast of Sukos, a difficulty which the Bible itself seems to experience. The explanation which the Bible gives is that when God brought the Israelites out of Egypt He made them dwell in booths seven days. "Ye shall dwell in booths seven days; all that are home-born in Israel shall dwell in booths; that your generations may know that I made the children of Israel to dwell in booths, when I brought them out of the land of Egypt: I am the Lord your God" (Lev. 23:42, 43). This festival has no specific phrase referring to this event but is merely described as the festival of Sukos, the time of our rejoicing.

In the Prayerbook the three festivals are treated as a group. The services for all of them are virtually alike except for rubrics in the form of a sentence or two indicating the characteristics of each holiday. There are also one or two special services for Passover and Tabernacles (the prayer for rain for Tabernacles and the prayer for dew for Passover), but, otherwise, all three services are identical. Each of the holidays has, of course, its own special reading from the Torah.

Passover, in Palestine and in Reform rituals, in accordance with biblical injunction, lasts for seven days and, in Babylon, for calendar reasons (see Chapter xx) for eight days. This is also the Orthodox custom. Sukos, in Palestine and in the Reform ritual, lasts for eight days and, in Babylon and in the Orthodox ritual, for nine days. In these two longer festivals the first day and the seventh day in Palestine for Passover and the first day and the eighth day for Sukos are full festivals; the intervening days are half-festivals (*chol hamo-ed*), "the profane days of the festival." In Babylon and in the Orthodox ritual, the first and the last two days of Passover and the first and the last two days of Sukos (namely, *Sh'mini Atseres* and *Simchas Torah*) are main holidays and the intervening days half-holidays. For the half-holidays there is a regular Week-day Service with a few special rubrics and small Torah sections dealing with the sacrifices of the holidays offered in the Temple and the recitation of the Hallel Psalms. These services need not be discussed in this chapter as they are identical with the daily services. Our concern is with the services of the main holidays.

The services of the main holidays are like the Sabbath Service in the following ways: the petitional prayers, the T'filo, do not have the thirteen intervening work-day petitions but in their place, similar to the Sabbath Service, there is only one intervening petition describing the holi-

day. Thus the T'filo has the regular three introductory and three concluding blessings, and with
the intervening blessing is a seven-blessing T'filo
like that of the Sabbath. It differs, however, from
the Sabbath in that, whereas the intervening
blessings in the three Sabbath T'filos differ from
one another, for morning, afternoon, and evening, the holiday T'filo is exactly the same except for a specific rubric now and then for each
Holiday Service. The Holiday Services and the
Sabbath Service are alike in that there are four
holiday T'filos as there are four Sabbath T'filos,
since there were additional sacrifices offered in
the Temple at Jerusalem for each holiday. As
mentioned before, the T'filos are understood to
correspond to the regular sacrifices, hence for the
additional sacrifices there is an additional Musof
T'filo. As on the Sabbath this Musof T'filo is
appended to the Morning Service and as in the
case of the Sabbath, is omitted in the Reform
rituals.

The services for the eve of every holiday are
like every Evening Service, primarily the Sh'ma
and its blessing (since the Sh'ma should be recited "when thou liest down"), and then a T'filo,
which unlike the other T'filos during the day,
is, as is the case with all evening services, not repeated aloud by the cantor or reader, since there
was no evening sacrifice in the Temple (Singer

Prayerbook, pp. 325-332; *Union Prayerbook*, pp. 181 ff.).

Before the close of the Evening Service (as is the case on the Sabbath), the Kiddush wine ceremony is recited, a custom introduced for the benefit of strangers who were often provided for in the synagogue if they had no other place to enjoy the festival meal. The only exception to this rule is on the first night of Passover when the Kiddush in the synagogue is omitted since every stranger in the city must be invited to a home to participate in the Passover Seder meal where he will hear the Kiddush as a home service. The Morning Service resembles the Sabbath Morning Service as to the chapters of psalms (P'sukei d'zimro). The extra psalms for the Sabbath are also recited on holidays (see Chapter xi). The Sh'ma and its blessings (the Yotser) are the same as on week-days. The T'filo is the special seven-blessing holiday T'filo, then follows the reading of the Torah as on Sabbath.

As for the reading of the Torah for the holidays, it differs from the reading on the Sabbath in this regard: the reading every Sabbath is part of the regular annual cycle (originally a triennial cycle in Palestine and in Egypt) and each week's portion begins where last week's portion ended, so that the entire Torah is read on the Sabbath throughout the year. But on the holidays a special reading which applies specifically to the holiday is selected. As a matter of fact, during the entire holiday the regular weekly portion is suspended, even for the Sabbath which comes within the holiday. Instead, a special holiday reading is provided, and if the Sabbath falls during the intervening half-holiday there is also read before the regular reading of the special Torah portion, the Book of Ecclesiastes on Sukos, the Song of Songs on Passover, and on Shovuos, where there is no half-holiday, the Book of Ruth on the second day. Thereafter, there follows on the last day of the holiday the memorial prayer (yizkor), also recited on the Day of Atonement. The Reform ritual omits this memorial prayer for Sukos and Shovuos, retaining it for the Day of Atonement and for the last day of Passover. Then in the Orthodox ritual, there follows the Musof T'filo and the close of the Service. The Afternoon Service, like any other Afternoon Service is primarily a T'filo, in this case a seven-blessing holiday T'filo. In addition to the prayers as outlined above, the Evening and Morning Services of the holidays were greatly amplified in medieval times by piyutim, liturgical poetry (discussed in Chapter XVII).

The joyous spirit of the festivals reaches out beyond the fixed synagogue liturgy. Each holiday has its additional avenues for the expression of its particular mood. Passover is especially marked by the Seder Service in the home, which vividly dramatizes the story of the deliverance from Egypt. Children and adults participate in reliving the experience of liberation. Thus, they obey year by year the rabbinic injunction that in every generation each person must consider that he personally has come out of Egyptian slavery (see also Chapter XVIII).

An especially joyous celebration developed during the Middle Ages for the last (the 9th) day of Sukos. This day, called *Simchas Torah*, the Rejoicing in the Law, marks the end of the yearly cycle of the consecutive Sabbath Torah readings. On the Sabbath after Sukos, the Torah reading begins again with the story of the Creation. Therefore, the last day of Sukos, the Rejoicing in the Law, is devoted to a celebration in honor of the Torah. On the evening before, and in the Morning Service itself, the scrolls are taken from the Ark and are carried in procession around the synagogue. In the Morning Service the man who is given the honor of reading the last section of Deuteronomy is called *Chasan Torah*, "the Bridegroom of the Law"; and the one who then reads the first verses from Genesis is called *Chasan B'reshis*, "the Bridegroom of the Beginning." The children march around the synagogue with their elders and are called up to the pulpit in a group for the reading of the Torah. The happy mood of the Torah celebration is voiced in the hymns written for it in the Middle Ages. Thus, for example,

This Feast of the Law all your gladness display,
  Today all your homages render.
What profit can lead one so pleasant a way,
  What jewels can vie with its splendor?
Then exult in the Law on its festival day,
  The Law is our Light and Defender.

My God I will praise in a jubilant lay,
  My hope in Him never surrender,
His glory proclaim where His chosen sons pray,
  My Rock all my trust shall engender.
Then exult in the Law on its festival day,
  The Law is our Light and Defender.

My heart of Thy goodness shall carol alway,
  Thy praises I ever will render;
While breath is, my lips all Thy wonders shall
    say,
  Thy truth and Thy kindness so tender.
Then exult in the Law on its festival day,
  The Law is our Light and Defender.

The following poem is based upon the midrashic legend that the Torah was preserved in heaven before it was given to Israel. The angels objected to having the Torah given away and they ask in this poem, referring to Moses, who is he that has come to take the Torah away from them?

The Angels came a-mustering,
   A-mustering, a-mustering,
The Angels came a-clustering
   Around the sapphire throne.

A-questioning of one another,
   Of one another, of one another,
A-questioning each one his brother
   Around the sapphire throne.

Pray who is he, and where is he,
   And where is he, and where is he,
Whose shining casts—so fair is he—
   A shadow on the throne?

Pray, who has up to heaven come,
   To heaven come, to heaven come,
Through all the circles seven come,
   To fetch the Torah down?

'Tis Moses up to heaven come,
   To heaven come, to heaven come,
Through all the circles seven come,
   To fetch the Torah down!

(Translations by Israel Zangwill, *Service of the Synagogue*, for Tabernacles, pp. 202-231.)

For over a century the festival of Shovuos has been enriched with the special ceremony of Confirmation. Confirmation, which began in Reform synagogues and was later adopted by most Conservative synagogues, is based upon the older rite of Bar Mitsvo. When a boy became thirteen years of age he was considered adult enough to be obligated to fulfil the religious commandments. As a symbol of his "coming of age," he was called to the Torah on the Sabbath nearest his thirteenth birthday. Confirmation differs from this older ceremony in that the children are often older than thirteen. They are usually fifteen or sixteen. Also, the ritual is not conducted for each child separately but for an entire group of boys and girls upon reaching the proper age. The day chosen for Confirmation, when a new generation accepts the Law of God, is quite appropriately the festival of Shovuos when Israel received the Law on Mount Sinai.

The Confirmation ritual is embodied into the Morning Service for Shovuos. The young people usually conduct the services and recite additional prayers and poems. The service ends with the rabbi bestowing a blessing upon each confirmand. The service is impressive both as a climax to the work of the religious school and as an enrichment of Shovuos, the ancient festival of the giving of the Law.

The spirit of the three festivals as expressed in the synagogue services is a blending of the two traditional moods: the year of nature as manifested in the harvest and the events of Israel's history. From these two, the mood of the festival is distilled—an emotion of sacred happiness as prescribed in the Bible: "And thou shalt be altogether joyful" (Deut. 16:15), "and thou shalt rejoice in thy feast" (Deut. 16:14). These biblical statements indicate an important element in the Judaism of the Prayerbook. Rejoicing at harvest is known among all peoples. Wild, hilarious, unruly festivals were found among all peoples at the important changes in the year's seasons. These hilarities were refined and ennobled in Israel by the understanding that the joy and the celebration were not mere outbursts of animal spirits but were ordained by God as a religious obligation.

How vast is the difference between the hilarity to which our animal nature impels us and the blessed joy which comes at the command of our Divine Father. Animal joy expresses itself, as indeed it did express itself in the harvest festivals of all people, in wild excesses of all kinds. Religious joy at the command of God was interwoven with ethical obligations. It was no longer selfish. It involved the responsibility that all who are around us shall rejoice with us. Furthermore, mere animal joy is a transient thing. If the harvest is a failure there will be no joy but sorrow. The mood of hilarity is quickly succeeded by a mood of deep depression. But when joy is looked upon as a religious duty, then it becomes a responsibility of man consciously to overcome his sorrow and despair. Even if the harvest be small and pitiable, he still thanks God for the blessings which he has received, for having kept him alive and brought him one season further along the road of life. Hence, the text of prayers always speaks of the fact that it is God who has given us these seasons of gladness, festivals, and seasons of joy (Singer *Prayerbook*, page 329). Also, "O Lord our God, bestow upon us the blessing of our appointed times for life and peace, for joy and gladness."

It is evident that what the synagogue accomplished with the Sabbath, it, likewise, achieved with the three harvest festivals. The Bible and after it the synagogue took the Sabbath idea of refraining from work, a negative idea of non-action, and converted it to a positive idea of spiritual repose and enrichment of soul. So did the Bible and the synagogue take the universal idea of hilarity at harvest time and convert it into a divinely ordained duty to rejoice with full heart and with generous sharing of God's gifts.

It is interesting to note how these two moods, the Sabbath of peace and the festival of happiness, are interwoven on the occasion when a festival happens to fall on a Sabbath. The phrases in the closing prayer of the T'filo weaves the two moods together like two separate melodies in harmony. "Bestow upon us the blessing of Thy season for joy and gladness." (For Sabbath, "Our God and God of our fathers, accept our rest.") "Satisfy us with Thy goodness, gladden us with Thy salvation, purify our hearts to serve Thee in truth. Let us inherit, O Lord our God (for Sabbath, 'in love and favor') with joy and gladness Thy holy (for Sabbath, 'and') appointed seasons." So, too, at the beginning of the intervening blessing in the T'filo, "Thou hast given us in love, O Lord, our God (Sabbath, 'for rest') festivals and seasons for joy." Sabbath rest is not idleness, it is serenity of the soul. The festival joy is not hilarity. It is radiance of life. Both are God-given.

·XIII·

The Book of Life

THE HIGH HOLIDAY SERVICE

THE New Year and the Day of Atonement are not primarily days of rejoicing but days of solemnity. They are devoted to earnest self-judgment in the presence of God, the eternal Judge. On these days each man searches out his inner failings, confesses the sins that he has committed, pleads before God for pardon, and hopes to reestablish his communion with the Father of Mercies. Each worshiper hopes to **rid** his heart of evil thoughts, to free his will from selfish desires. He endeavors, as far as fallible man can do so, to become holy as God is holy. In sharp contrast to the joyous mood of the three pilgrim festivals (Passover, Shovuos, and Sukos), the first ten days of the month of *Tishri*, beginning with the New Year (Rosh Ha-shono), followed by the Days of Penitence, and concluding with the Day of Atonement (Yom Kippur), are known in the Prayerbook as "Awesome Days" (Yomim Noro-im).

The first of these days, New Year, is almost entirely the product of the Synagogue and the Prayerbook. It is astonishing how little of the spirit of the day is derived from the Bible itself. Leviticus (23:23-25) speaks only of refraining from work, and holding a sacred gathering, and blowing the trumpet. "In the seventh month, in the first day of the month, shall be a solemn rest unto you, a memorial proclaimed with the blast of horns, a holy convocation. Ye shall do no manner of servile work; and ye shall bring an offering made by fire unto the Lord." The Book of Numbers (29:1-6) speaks of the holiday in the same meager terms, giving somewhat more detail of the sacrificial requirements. In Nehemiah (8) we are told that Nehemiah and Ezra read the Law to the people on the first day of the seventh month. These leaders told the people, "this day is holy unto the Lord your God, mourn not, nor weep." This is virtually the entire biblical material dealing with the New Year. Upon the basis of these few ideas, a day of rest, sounding of the trumpet, and convocation, the entire New Year Service is built. Not only does the Prayerbook amplify these few formal ideas but it brings entirely new ideas into the service. These new ideas are beautifully elaborated in prose and poetry. Judging by the Bible the first day of *Tishri* was of very little importance.

Judging by the Prayerbook we see that it has become one of the greatest spiritual influences in the life of Israel.

As with all days of the year the New Year Service begins the evening before. The Evening Service is similar to all other Evening Services but the petitional prayer (the T'filo) is characteristic of the day. It is, of course (as are all Sabbath and holiday T'filos), different from the daily T'filo in that it consists of seven blessings except in the additional service (the Musof), which, because of the Service of the Trumpet (the Shofor), has nine blessings. That is to say, the daily thirteen requests for the needs of every day are omitted, and in their place there is one benediction descriptive of the festival.

While the three introductory benedictions of the T'filo, (a) God of Abraham, Isaac, and Jacob, (b) God's might, (c) God's holiness, are the same essentially as all through the year in every T'filo, the third of these three introductory benedictions, "God's holiness," is magnificently amplified for the New Year and also for the Day of Atonement. In this third benediction the universalistic mood of the High Holy days finds noble expression. We ask that God impose the reverence for Him not only upon the heart of His worshipers, the children of Israel, but upon the heart of all mankind, so that all God's children may unite to form one brotherhood with perfect heart, and that God vindicate the hope of all who seek Him so that the dominion of wickedness and arrogance shall pass away from the earth and God alone shall reign as King. This sublime prayer, inserted in the third introductory benediction of every T'filo of the High Holidays, is one of the high points of the entire Prayerbook (Singer *Prayerbook*, page 350; *Union Prayerbook*,* II, 58).

The fourth or intervening benediction describing the holiday, is much like the intervening blessing describing the three pilgrim festivals except that its closing paragraph contains a more specific reference to the High Holidays. Thus, while for the pilgrim festivals the Prayerbook asks, "Bestow upon us the blessing of Thy appointed times for joy and gladness, satisfy us with Thy goodness, gladden us with Thy salvation, let us inherit O Lord our God with joy and gladness Thy holy season," the High Holiday blessing returns to the noble universal note of the third introductory benediction, quoted above in the prayer: "Our God and God of our fathers, reign Thou in glory, over the whole universe, so that whatsoever hath been created may understand that Thou hast created it, and all that have breath may say: 'The Lord God of Is-

* Revised Edition.

rael is King and His dominion ruleth over all.' "
(Cf. Singer *Prayerbook*, page 353 with 344. In
Union Prayerbook, cf. I, 228, bottom, with
Union Prayerbook, II, 58, last paragraph.)

The Morning Service of the New Year is
richly developed. The chapters of Psalms and
the blessings around the Sh'ma (the Yotser) are
much like the Sabbath. The T'filo is like the
New Year's Eve T'filo, except that it ends with
the petitional litany: "Our Father, our King, we
have sinned before Thee, etc." (*Service of the
Synagogue*, for the New Year, page 111; *Union
Prayerbook*, II, 64, 31). There is a special Torah
reading for the New Year. In the Orthodox
ritual, the first day has a selection from Genesis
(21), the birth of Isaac, and on the second day
the continuation of the story, the sacrifice of
Isaac. The Reform ritual, which observes one
day, has as its Torah reading the sacrifice of
Isaac. The prophetical portion in the Orthodox
ritual for the first day, the birth of Samuel, is
the same in the Reform ritual.

The great addition to the Torah service on
the New Year's Day is the sounding of the trumpet (the Shofor). The Orthodox Service has the
Shofor ritual in two places in the New Year
Service, first after the reading of the Torah and
then also in the T'filo for the additional service
(Musof). The Reform ritual, which does not

have the Musof Service, concentrates the Shofor ritual after the Torah reading.

The sounding of the trumpet which, according to the Bible, marks the beginning of every
month, is of course prescribed for this seventh
month also. Of this simple ritual requirement the
Prayerbook has made an elaborate and inspiring
ceremony. Not only is the Shofor sounded
but elaborate prayers are developed to explain
the meaning and to intensify the effect of the
trumpet blasts. In order to achieve this aim,
verses were selected from the Bible and rear-
ranged into three groups. The first verses deal
with the universalistic concept of God the King
of all the world and are headed *Malchiyos*, from
the word *Melech*, meaning "King." The second
group uses the thought of God's remembering
the events of history, and, hence, knowing all
things past, present, and future, God is described
as the righteous Judge of all mankind since nothing is hidden from His sight. This group is headed
Zichronos from the root *zochar*, meaning "to
remember." The third group of verses deals with
the trumpet of deliverance, the sound of the
trumpet first heard on Mount Sinai, and the
trumpet of deliverance that shall sound in the
future. This group is called *Shoforos*, from the
word for trumpet, Shofor. All the trumpet
blasts which are sounded after each group of

prayers is recited conclude with the statement that this day is like the creation of the world. On this day all the world, new-born, stands before God's judgment throne, and God will deal mercifully with mankind as a father pitieth his children. (*Union Prayerbook*, II, 75 to 81; *Service of the Synagogue*, pp. 126, 127, for the Shofor Service after the Torah, and pp. 125-162, for the Shofor Service during the Musof.) As is the case with the festival service, later generations, particularly in medieval times, greatly elaborated most of the service with hymns and poems.

The main spiritual achievement of the Prayerbook in the New Year Service is that it combines the universalistic passages scattered through prophetic writing with the sound of the Shofor which is prescribed rather dryly and without elaboration in the Torah itself. The highest vision of the prophets was that all mankind are children of one Father, that they are destined some day to realize their brotherhood, that they will someday beat their swords into ploughshares, cease fratricidal strife, and form one united family, worshipping one God. This exalted vision running through prophetic literature was so far in advance of the actual experiences of daily life that it might easily have remained mere literary imagination, occasionally impressing some few choice spirits. But the Prayerbook took up this vision and saved it from becoming a transient dream. This vision, beautified and elaborated, became a living element in the hope of every humble worshiper. If the hope for universal peace buoyed up the people of Israel through all the long centuries of bloody warfare, if the confidence of a future human unity gave patience and stamina to a hopeless minority in a world of race and national hatred, it was because the dream of the prophets was translated into a regular part of Jewish worship. Thus, even in the Dark Ages, when the dreams of the prophets might have seemed so hopelessly remote, the universalism of the New Year Service continued to inspire creative poetry in this vein. The following poem written in the midst of the Dark Ages for the New Year Service, illustrates how creative an impulse this universal hope had become in Jewish life.

All the world shall come to serve Thee
    And bless Thy Glorious Name,
And Thy righteousness triumphant
    The islands shall acclaim.
And the peoples shall go seeking
    Who knew Thee not before,
And the ends of earth shall praise Thee
    And tell Thy greatness o'er.
They shall build for Thee their altars,
    Their idols overthrown,
And their graven gods shall shame them,
    As they turn to Thee alone.

They shall worship Thee at sunrise,
    And feel Thy Kingdom's might,
And impart their understanding
    To those astray in night.

As part of the prophetic vision in the Bible
that the day of human peace and reunion will
come, the prophets and psalmists speak of God's
great day of judgment in the future. God will
judge all mankind, and after this inevitable judgment, men will realize their iniquity and return
to God united. This judgment scene bound up
with the coming of the universal unity of man
is also transformed in the New Year Service.
Instead of the concept of some distant day of
world judgment the Prayerbook makes the New
Year Day an annual day of judgment. The idea
is summed up in the Mishnah (m. Rosh Ha-
shono, 1, 2): on the New Year Day all human
beings pass before God to be counted like sheep
by their shepherd. God's decision as to the good
and evil practiced by men and nations is not
postponed to a far-off day but becomes a living
reality year after year. God is the Judge of mankind and His judgment becomes clear every
New Year's Day. The poetic fancy of the people elaborated the thought of God's annual judgment of all men, envisioning the record books of
the judge in which decisions are written down.
Thus they describe three books (b. Rosh Ha-

shono 16b), open before God on New Year's Day, in which are written down the righteous, the wicked, and the intermediate. Hence, the insertion in the New Year T'filos and during the ten days of penitence of prayers that God "write us down in the Book of Life." The older poetic descriptions of God's judgment serve the modern worshiper as symbolic expression of his own self-judgment in the presence of God. Each man weighs his own life in the scale of God's balance. He knows that the vision of an ennobled and united humanity will remain a mere vision until it is built upon the foundation of a purified human character.

This, then, is the great achievement of the New Year Service; out of a few simple biblical descriptions it made a powerful sublime liturgy. From the prophetic idea that some day God would judge the earth and His judgment eventuate in a united mankind, the Prayerbook developed the idea of the call of the trumpet, summoning mankind year by year to God's judgment throne, and making the vision of humanity ennobled and reunited, a living theme in every life.

* * *

The Day of Atonement has a much wider biblical basis than New Year's Day. The ritual prescribed in the Five Books of Moses for this day indicates that already in earlier years its great significance was stressed. The Bible in Leviticus (16), lists all the elaborate offerings for atonement which the High Priest must make. The garments which he must wear are described, and we are told that he must atone for the Temple itself, for the priesthood, and for the people. In Leviticus (23:27-32), immediately following the brief statement concerning the New Year, considerable detail is given about the observance of the Day of Atonement. There is the same requirement as on the New Year for abstinence from work and for gathering in holy convocation, but in addition it is said, "Ye shall afflict your souls . . . for it is a Day of Atonement for you before the Lord your God." It is also called the Sabbath of solemn rest or the Sabbath of Sabbaths.

The Mishnah in Tractate Yomo indicates clearly how important the Day of Atonement was in the ritual of the Temple at Jerusalem. The ceremonies conducted by the High Priest are here given in greater detail: his sacrifices and the text of his three confessions (for his own household, for the priesthood, and for the household of Israel). During these confessions as the people crowded the courts and heard the name of God, they prostrated themselves and they said, "Blessed be the name of His glory forever."

In all this ceremonial splendor in the Temple on the Day of Atonement, it is to be noticed that the participation of the people was almost nil. They were present; they watched the ritual; and during the confessions by the High Priest, uttered their pious phrase praising God. But in the synagogue there gradually developed a richly elaborated, profoundly moving service. The mood of the service in the Temple was that the priest, through the prescribed ritual, made atonement for the people. The people were passive beneficiaries of the elaborate Temple ceremony of atonement. But in the synagogue where the people were the active participants in worship, the mood was that each person by his own sincerity of thought made atonement for himself. The Day of Atonement prayers were directed to the achievement of self-purification. They have served this spiritual purpose throughout the centuries.

The Evening Service of the Day of Atonement is much like the Evening Service for the New Year except that in later centuries it began with the famous prayer, Kol Nidrei, calling for the release from those ritual vows which had been hastily made (see Chapter XIV). The petitional prayer (the T'filo) is virtually identical with that of the New Year. It has the same insertions, asking God to write us in the Book of Life. The third introductory blessing of God's holiness contains the New Year's universalistic prayer that God put reverence for Him into the hearts of men, that all may unite into one brotherhood, and that the dominion of arrogance pass from the earth. The fourth (intervening) blessing is, except for a phrase or two, identical with that of the New Year. At the conclusion of the Day of Atonement T'filos, there is a series of confessions for the sins "which we have sinned against Thee under compulsion or of free will, etc." (*Service of the Synagogue*, for Eve of Atonement, page 26; *Union Prayerbook*, II, 117).

The Morning Service of the Day of Atonement is much like the Morning Service for the New Year, but with a greater number of prayers of confession and supplication particularly in the repetition of the T'filo by the reader. The special Torah reading from Leviticus (16), describes the ritual of the Day of Atonement, and the prophetical portion, from Isaiah 57 and 58, describes the ethical implications of sincere fasting (see also Chapter IX). After the Torah reading the Orthodox Service has here the Memorial Service (see Chapter XII). The Reform ritual moves the Memorial Service to later in the afternoon. The Musof Service is greatly elaborated.

Its chief content is a vivid and powerful elaboration of the description of the ritual of the High Priest in the Temple on the Day of Atonement. This description, based upon Leviticus (17), and upon the Mishnah Tractate Yomo, depicts the whole priestly service step by step. When the priest made his confession the people in the Temple courts prostrated themselves and said, "Praised be the Name of His Glory forever." At this point in the synagogue service the people in the congregation (as did their ancestors in the Temple) kneel and repeat the same sentence.

The Afternoon Service is like the Afternoon Service for other days and for the New Year. Its chief characteristic is that the Torah is read before the T'filo as on the Sabbath inasmuch as the Day of Atonement is considered a Sabbath, indeed the Sabbath of Sabbaths. The reading is from Leviticus (18) in the Orthodox ritual; and in the *Union Prayerbook* from Exodus (33-34). The prophetical reading is the biblical Book of Jonah, an appropriate selection, since the theme of the Book of Jonah is repentance. Furthermore, the Book fits into the universalistic note of the High Holiday season inasmuch as it deals with the repentance of a pagan city, the city of Nineveh, and proves that all who come to God in sincere repentance will be received in forgiveness.

After the Afternoon Service, Yom Kippur has a fourth service, the N'ilo, the service of the closing of the gates. The N'ilo Service corresponds to the closing of the gates in the Temple at Jerusalem. The *Ma-a-modos*, the committees of the people who twice a year spent a week in the Temple at Jerusalem representing their districts, prayed four times each day, the first three services corresponded to sacrifices (morning, additional, and afternoon, and the fourth at the closing of the gates). In the ancient fast-day services there was also a service for the closing of the gates. Now this gate-closing service remains in the Jewish Prayerbook only on the Day of Atonement. This service is constructed much like an Afternoon Service, consisting chiefly of a T'filo. The T'filo is like the regular Day of Atonement T'filo except that now that the day is virtually over and the atonement, we hope, granted, the worshiper, instead of saying, "Write us in the Book of Life," says, "Seal us in the Book of Life." Also the confessions of sin are now largely abbreviated. The entire atonement service is greatly elaborated by medieval poetry. Inasmuch as the service lasts all day there is ample time for additional poetry;

the medieval poets, therefore, lavished great skill and invention on this day's service.

The Day of Atonement provides a fitting climax to the spirit of the entire penitential season. The great world vision of New Year's Day, wherein God judges all of mankind and holds before His children the picture of a united humanity, will remain unattainable as long as the individual man allows selfishness and injustice to dominate his personal life. The Mishnah says that before the Day of Atonement can effect purification of the heart, man must first undo whatever ill he has done to his fellow man. Only then can he hope that the estrangement which has grown up between him and God may perhaps be bridged. Thus, on the Day of Atonement man seeks, by excluding himself from the outer world, spending the day in the sanctuary, deepening his spiritual emotions by poetry, prayer, and song, to come near to the Divine Presence. As each Day of Atonement's task is done, to whatever extent it has been accomplished, to that extent man's individual life receives an added touch of nobility and the dream of a New Year in which the nations' mutual bitterness will be diminished, is brought nearer to fulfilment.

·XIV·

I Turn to Thee

SPECIAL PRAYERS

CERTAIN prayers have won a special place in the affections of Jewish worshipers. The ideas expressed in them have had an important influence upon the state of mind of the average Jew. A study of these special prayers can serve as an exemplification of the central ideas in the liturgy.

A. The Priestly Blessing. One of the most solemn prayers in the entire Prayerbook ritual is the blessing of the people by the descendants of Aaron (the *Kohanim*, the priests). This ritual is one of the oldest elements in the service and is one of the few prayer texts prescribed in the Bible. In Numbers (6:23-27) the priests are commanded: "On this wise ye shall bless the children of Israel; ye shall say unto them: the Lord bless thee, and keep thee; the Lord make His face to shine upon thee, and be gracious unto thee; the Lord lift up His countenance upon thee, and give thee peace. So shall they put My name upon

the children of Israel, and I will bless them."
II Chronicles (30:27) records, "Then the priests
the Levites arose and blessed the people."

From the old Temple ritual as it is given to
us in the Mishnah and other talmudic literature
we have a clear picture of how and when this
blessing was given. In connection with the regular daily offering the priests would go to the
platform (*duchon*) which stood three steps
higher than the court of Israel and there pronounce the blessing. Since there were two regular daily offerings this blessing was generally
recited twice a day, but on holidays when there
was an additional offering (Musof), it was recited
also in connection with this offering. On fast-
days and in connection with the committees of
laymen, the *Ma-a-modos*, it was recited also at
the closing of the gates (N'ilo). Thus, there
were occasions when the priestly blessing was
recited four times in one day at the Temple.

Later, it became customary for the priests to
recite this blessing in the various synagogues all
over the land. Inasmuch as there were always
priests available in every town (only one
"watch," one twenty-fourth of the priesthood,
officiated each week in Jerusalem), this was not
difficult to arrange. Inasmuch as the petitional
prayer, the T'filo, was considered to parallel the
regular offerings in the Temple, the priestly bless-

ing was appended to the daily T'filo. Originally, the priests blessed the people at the close of the T'filo of every service, i.e., Morning and Afternoon Services. Later, this was restricted to a priestly blessing only in the Morning Service. This still remains the custom in certain parts of the world as for example in Yemen (southern Arabia). Still later the blessing by the priest was restricted to the Sabbath and holidays, which was the custom of the Spanish ritual. Then, particularly in northern Europe, it was restricted to holidays only.

The present Orthodox custom is that on every holiday at the close of the additional T'filo, the Musof (except when the holiday happens to fall on the Sabbath), the priests, descendants of Aaron, ascend the platform and repeat after the cantor the priestly blessing, word for word. The service is invested with great solemnity. The priests cover their heads with their praying shawls, hold their hands high in front of them, spreading their fingers in the prescribed manner, and with plaintive chant repeat each word of the blessing. This blessing by the priests is one of the few remaining privileges of the descendants of Aaron since the destruction of the Temple, another being the right to be the first of the seven men called up on the Sabbath to the reading of the Torah. In the Reform ritual, which does not recognize any distinction between priests, Levites, and Israelites, the priestly blessing is recited by the reader whatever be his special lineage. (*Union Prayerbook*, page 240, beginning, "Our God and God of our fathers . . ."; *Service of the Synagogue*, for Passover, page 152, and in the corresponding place in the other holiday volumes.)

Inasmuch as the priestly blessing originally took place every day and not merely on holidays, a residue of the older custom remains in the daily service. Towards the close of the T'filo, after the second of the three concluding blessings, the reader himself, whether he be priest or Levite or Israelite, recites the priestly blessing.

In the original Temple service this blessing was felt to have somewhat of a magic power to ward off evil, particularly since the ineffable name of God was pronounced in the original way (i.e., as it was written). The rabbis, however, are very careful to explain that it is not the priests who bless the people, but God who blesses the people. Indeed, this is indicated in the verse which follows the priestly blessing in Numbers (6:27), "So shall they put My name upon the children of Israel, and I will bless them." The rabbis emphasized the word "I"; God says, "*I* will bless the people." Nevertheless, the sense that the Divine Presence hovered around the priest during the blessing, gave rise to the prohibition of looking at the priests at that time lest the eye of the beholder be dazzled and dimmed.

However, all these semi-magical ideas are of small importance compared with the content of the blessing itself, particularly as it was elaborated by rabbinical interpretation. The words, "The Lord bless thee," are understood to mean that God grant prosperity; "and keep thee," means the blessing of health; "make His face to shine upon thee," means the Divine Presence may be radiant over thee; "and be gracious unto thee," to grant thee knowledge and instruction and wisdom. The final blessing, "and give thee peace," received warm comment on the part of the rabbinical writers. Peace is described in panegyric terms as the greatest of all blessings, as God's special and favorite blessing.

Since the whole benediction climaxes with the hope and yearning for peace, the closing word and thought of the blessing, "Peace," was elaborated into a complete and separate prayer, "Grant us peace," which became the closing prayer of the T'filo. (Singer *Prayerbook*, page 65. "Grant peace . . . every hour with thy peace." *Union Prayerbook*, page 140.) In fact, this prayer, "Grant us peace," is still known in the rabbinical writings as the "blessing of the priests," thus revealing its original connection with the closing phrase of the priestly blessing which precedes it. The text in the *Union Prayerbook*, while a paraphrase, expresses the mood of the prayer: "Grant us peace, Thy most precious gift, O Thou eternal source of peace, and enable Israel to be its messenger unto the peoples of the earth. Bless our country that it may ever be a stronghold of peace, and its advocate in the council of nations. May contentment reign within its borders, health and happiness within its homes. Strengthen the bonds of friendship and fellowship among all the inhabitants of our land. Plant virtue in every soul and may the love of Thy name hallow every home and every heart. Praised be Thou, O Lord, Giver of Peace."

B. Adoration (*Olenu*). At the end of each one of the three daily services is found one of the most sublime prayers in the entire Prayerbook. This prayer, generally called Olenu ("It is our duty") from its opening words, or "Adoration" in the Reform ritual because of its essential theme, expresses a lofty spiritual and social mood. (Singer *Prayerbook*, page 93, "It is our duty to praise the Lord of all things," to page 94, "the Lord shall be One, and his name One." And at the end of each service, *Union Prayerbook*, page 71, "Let us adore the ever-living God," to page 72, "His Name shall be One," and so at the end of every other service.) The text of this prayer as given in the *Union Prayerbook* (somewhat paraphrased from the text in the Orthodox Prayerbook) is as follows:

"Let us adore the ever-living God, and render praise unto Him who spread out the heavens and established the earth, whose glory is revealed in the heavens above and whose greatness is manifest throughout the world. He is our God; there is none else.

"We bow the head in reverence, and worship the King of kings, the Holy One, praised be He.

"May the time not be distant, O God, when Thy name shall be worshipped in all the earth, when unbelief shall disappear and error be no more. Fervently we pray that the day may come when all men shall invoke Thy name, when corruption and evil shall give way to purity and goodness, when superstition shall no longer enslave the mind, nor idolatry blind the eye, when all who dwell on earth shall know that to Thee alone every knee must bend and every tongue give homage. O may all, created in Thine image, recognize that they are brethren, so that, one in spirit and one in fellowship, they may be forever united before Thee. Then shall Thy kingdom be established on earth and the word of Thine ancient seer be fulfilled: the Lord will reign forever and ever.

"On that day the Lord shall be One and His name shall be One."

There is no evidence that this sublime adoration of God's greatness and unity was recited at the end of the daily prayers before the twelfth century. The earlier authorities do not know of it as the close of the service. Its original place is in the Musof Service (additional service) of the New Year where it is the introduction to the Shofor ritual. The first part of the Shofor ritual, Malchiyos, "God as King" (see Chapter XIII) emphasizes God as the Lord of all mankind and stresses the universal note inherent in the Shofor ritual. To this universal idea the Adoration prayer is a fitting introduction. It speaks of God Who alone must be adored in human worship. It declares the nothingness of idolatry and idols and ends with the hope that all men will some day abandon their paganism and worship God alone. "On that day the Lord shall be One and His Name shall be One."

Because this prayer is so suitable as an introduction to the Shofor Service many scholars have come to the conclusion that it was written by Rav, the third century Babylonian rabbi, to whom the authorship of the Shofor ritual is ascribed. Other scholars say that it is far older than that. Its stress on the sin of idolatry, the fact that it is virtually a mosaic of great prophetic utterances, points to an older origin, long before the destruction of the Temple. (See Kohler, *Jewish Encyclopedia*, I, 337; and Kohler, *Origins of Synagogue and Church*, pp. 100-102.) It is interesting to note how much of the text of this prayer comes from the great anti-idolatry preachments of the prophets. A mere citation of the prophetic verses used will reveal that fact clearly (Jer. 10:6 ff.): "There is none like unto Thee, O Lord; Thou art great, and Thy name is great in might. . . . Forasmuch as among all the wise men of the nations, and in all their royalty, there is none like unto Thee. . . . But the Lord God is the true God, He is the living God, and the everlasting King." Compare the following sentence, Singer *Prayerbook*, page 93, "He hath not made us like the nations of other lands (i.e., the pagan idolators) . . . he hath not assigned unto us a portion as unto them, for we bend the knee and offer worship before the supreme King of kings." Compare this with Jeremiah (10:16), "Not like these is the portion of Jacob; for He is the former of all things, and Israel is the tribe of His inheritance; the Lord of hosts is His name." And so on through the prayer to the closing thought which ends with the verse from Zechariah (14:9), "And the Lord shall be King over all the earth; in that day shall the Lord be One and His name One."

This prayer, completely biblical in tone, voices the great struggle for monotheism, so typical of the message of the prophets. It may well be very old but it found its way into the regular ritual first, as we have said, in connection with the service of sounding the trumpet on the New Year, in honor of God the King. Eventually, this prayer was brought out of the context of the New Year prayers and used as the close of every daily service, indicating that in Jewish prayer the hope that idolatry and superstition will vanish and that all men will worship God alone, was considered to be the climax of the entire worship.

It is a curious and disheartening fact that this noble prayer became the unjust cause of considerable persecution of the Jew, chiefly due to Jewish apostates who claimed that the prayer was anti-Christian. In the original version of the prayer there was a sentence referring to the idolators, "They worship that which is vain and of no purpose" (Isa. 30:7). The apostates said that the Hebrew word for "no purpose" adds up numerically to the name "Jesus," and hence the Jews prayed daily against the Christian savior. The charge was, of course, absurd. Even if the prayer were written at the latest assignable date, namely, by Rav in Babylon in the third century, that teacher, in a Persian Zoroastrian environment, would hardly have written a prayer against Christianity. In all likelihood, he never saw a Christian. Besides, it may well be that the prayer is much older and pre-Christian. It denounces not Christianity but idolatry and the phrase containing the word which is supposed to be a disguised attack on Jesus comes from Isaiah, who lived centuries before the Christian era. In spite of the absurdity of these attacks the sentence was finally omitted from all rituals.

The important fact concerning the Adoration is that this great prayer was placed at the close of each day's service. The Jewish ritual reveals its true tendency in this fact. Each service must end with the hope that superstition will disappear and idolatry be no more, that all mankind will acknowledge their common brotherhood under God's Fatherhood. That is the constant refrain and the firm hope of the Jewish service.

C. *Kaddish.* Following the Adoration in every service is a prayer greatly beloved by the Jewish worshiper, the Kaddish prayer in honor of the departed. This prayer is in its original forms very ancient, although its modern usage as a prayer in honor of the departed is not older than the thirteenth century. The kernel of the prayer is the congregational response after the first paragraph, "May His great Name be blessed forever and ever." This response not only expresses the basic purpose of the prayer but is also its oldest element and around this response the whole prayer gradually developed. This phrase, praising God, is, like most of the Kaddish, in Aramaic, and is found almost verbatim in the Book of Daniel (2:20), "And Daniel spoke and said: Blessed be the name of God from everlasting even unto everlasting." In its Hebrew form the same verse is found in Psalm 113:2. It will be noticed that the phrase resembles the one which the people recited in the Temple at Jerusalem when they prostrated themselves at the mention by the priests of the Ineffable Name, namely, "Blessed be the Name of His glory, forever and ever." The latter phrase likewise has a permanent part in the Prayerbook as a response to "Hear O Israel, the Lord our God the Lord is One."

This response in the Kaddish was praised highly by the rabbis and greatly revered, being described as one of the "pillars of the world" (b. Sota 49a). And (in b. B'rochos 3a) we are told that "when the people enter the synagogues and schools and respond, 'may His Great Name be praised, etc.,' God, as it were, nods His head and says: blessed be the King Who is so praised in His house." The original use of this prayer seems to have been in the schools or in the synagogue when the synagogue was used as a school or a house of study. After study was completed for the day someone would arise and utter a prayer calling for God's deliverance and the coming of the Messiah; then the people would respond, "May the great Name be praised forever and ever." The first paragraph of the Kaddish which is messianic, is the prayer that was thus recited to which the response was made. This first paragraph with the response is the older part of this prayer. The "Lord's Prayer" of the Gospels is clearly based upon it as can be seen readily from a translation. The opening paragraph reads: "May the great Name be magnified and hallowed in the world which He has created by His will and may His kingdom reign in your life and in the life of all Israel soon. Amen." This is clearly the source of "our Father, hallowed be Thy name, may Thy kingdom come and Thy will be done."

In the Orthodox ritual this prayer is still used after study and is also read at various dividing points of the service. Thus after the morning psalms (P'sukei d'zimro) the reader recites a form of the Kaddish (called Half-Kaddish). At the close of the Morning Service before the Adoration (Olenu), the reader recites another form of the Kaddish called the full Kaddish. After the Adoration the mourners recite the mourner's Kaddish.

In ancient times the custom of mourners to say Kaddish for their departed relatives was unknown. It was only in northern Europe in the period of persecution, the twelfth and thirteenth centuries, that it became the general custom for mourners to honor their departed parents by reciting this prayer in the presence of the congregation.

Essentially the prayer neither in its origin nor in its thought has anything to do with a prayer for the dead, except insofar as its general tone is one of praise of God and the acceptance of His Will. Inasmuch as the first paragraph contains a hope for God's messianic kingdom to be established on earth, perhaps the idea was of especial consolation to the bereaved, particularly since in former times it was held that the coming of the Messiah was to be preceded by the resurrection of the dead.

It is significant that in the Jewish Prayerbook the prayer which became associated with the departed is one of serene acceptance of the Divine Will and as such has helped strengthen the bereaved and the heavy-laden. The *Union Prayerbook* provides special introductory prayers before the Kaddish expressing the acceptance of God's Will and voicing words of consolation. The following prayer (page 72) expresses the mood found in most of them:

"All you who mourn the loss of loved ones, and, at this hour, remember the sweet companionship and the cherished hopes that have passed away with them, give ear to the word of comfort spoken in the name of God. Only the body has died and has been laid in the dust. The spirit lives in the shelter of God's love and mercy. Our loved ones continue, also, in the remembrance of those to whom they were precious. Their deeds of lovingkindness, the true and beautiful words they spoke are treasured up as incentives to conduct by which the living honor the dead. And when we ask in our grief: Whence shall come our help and our comfort? then in the strength of faith let us answer with the Psalmist: My help cometh from God. He will not forsake us nor leave us in our grief. Upon Him we cast our burden and He will grant us strength according to the days He has apportioned to us. All life comes from Him; all souls are in His keeping. Come then, and in the midst of sympathizing fellow-worshipers, rise and hallow the name of God."

D. Kol Nidrei. One of the most famous rituals of the synagogue is conducted at the beginning of the service for the eve of the Day of Atonement, the Kol Nidrei. The preparations for the prayer are solemn. Two leaders of the congregation each take a scroll from the Ark and then take their places on each side of the cantor who, with a much beloved famous melody, recites the prayer. The prayer is in Aramaic and is nothing more or less than a legal formula asking for the release of vows made from this Day of Atonement to the next. The text as found in the Orthodox ritual is as follows (*Service of the Synagogue*, Eve of Atonement, page 15): "All vows, bonds, oaths, devotions, promises, penalties and obligations: wherewith we have vowed, sworn, devoted and bound ourselves: from this Day of Atonement unto the next Day of Atonement, may it come unto us for good: lo, all these, we repent us of them. They shall be absolved, released, annulled, made void, and of none effect: they shall not be binding nor shall they have any power. Our vows shall not be vows: our bonds shall not be bonds: and our oaths shall not be oaths."

This prayer, like the Adoration, has been the cause of considerable persecution of the Jews. On the basis of this prayer slanderers have said that the promises and oaths taken by a Jew are not to be trusted because on the Day of Atonement he declares them all null and void beforehand. Of course, this is either a horrible misunderstanding or a cruel libel. The prayer does not refer to any vows or promises made by a man in relation to other human beings. All our debts and promises to our fellow men must be fulfilled before the Day of Atonement can bring atonement to us. The Mishnah (m. Yomo VIII, 9) says that the Day of Atonement can bring forgiveness for the sins in the relation of man to God; but sins of man against man can never be forgiven on the Day of Atonement unless man make up the wrong that he has done to his fellow.

The first part of the statement in the Mishnah explains the meaning of the Kol Nidrei formula; it refers to vows made in the relation of man to God, that is to say, vows that man made with regard to himself in relation to God. In ancient times the Jews were very prone to make hasty ritual vows: to bring sacrifices, to fast, or to impose penance on themselves. All these vows must be fulfilled but if a man makes such a ritual vow hastily or carelessly the vow still remains in force unless he can find release from it. Part of the function of the rabbis in older days was to help achieve release from some of these hasty ritual vows. Because vows may be hastily made and then perhaps forgotten and no release formally obtained for them, the people ask now that whatever hasty ritual promise they made in relation to God, may be released so that they may begin the day with a clear conscience.

Although this formula had nothing to do with vows between man and man, nevertheless, a vast array of rabbinical authority since ancient time (since the eighth century when the prayer was first heard of) protested against this blanket release even from ritual vows, but the presence of the prayer in the ritual is a proof that the desire of the people overcame even the objection of the formal authorities. So eager were they for "clean hands and a pure heart" that they wanted to be sure that their hasty religious promises should not remain either unfulfilled or unreleased. Nowadays the great appeal of the prayer is not so much in the Aramaic legal formula or its meaning but in its sublime melody. In Reform rituals where a poem or a formula of a more spiritual nature is substituted for the original legal formula, the same inspiring melody is retained.

XV

I Will Sing unto the Lord

HYMNS IN THE PRAYERBOOK

DURING the Middle Ages a vast amount of poetic material found its way into the Prayerbook particularly into the service of the festivals and the High Holidays (see Chapter XVII). These poems varied from country to country and even from city to city. The Spanish ritual had an entirely different set of poems from that of the German and the German differed completely from the Italian, etc. There are, however, four hymns which became common to virtually all the rituals and were used at least every week and some of them every day. These popular hymns inspired many cantors and musicians to set the poems to music so that there are numerous melodies available for them. A study of the thoughts expressed in these four hymns should indicate which religious ideas have appealed most strongly to all Jewish worshipers.

A. Ein Kelohenu. The title of the first of these hymns is taken from its opening words, *Ein*

Kelohenu, "There is none like our God." This hymn is found in all rituals, the Spanish Jew reciting it every day and the North European, the German, reciting it on the Sabbath at the close of the service. It is not possible to date this hymn exactly inasmuch as the author is unknown. It is quoted in the Prayerbook of the Gaon Amram, who lived in the ninth century.

The phraseology of the hymn is not particularly beautiful; in fact, it is rather repetitious like a litany. Perhaps this simplicity helped keep it easily in the memory while the significant ideas which it conveyed made it worth remembering. The text of the hymn is as follows:

> There is none like our God,
> There is none like our Lord,
> There is none like our King,
> There is none like our Savior.
>
> Who is like our God,
> Who is like our Lord, etc.
>
> Let us give thanks unto our God,
> Let us give thanks unto our Lord, etc.
>
> Blessed be our God,
> Blessed be our Lord, etc.

It is evident that there is no particular beauty of diction in this hymn. Therefore, the fact that it became so widespread and has been maintained in all the prayerbooks for eleven centuries or more, must be due to its essential idea. The hymn is primarily a description of God and man's duty to Him, a theme which is expressed by two of the other popular prayerbook hymns to be discussed in this chapter. The Jewish concept of God is revealed in the very succession of names applied to Him in each line of the hymn. The words "Our God" (*Elohenu*), "Our Lord" (*Adonenu*), "Our King" (*Malchenu*), "Our Savior" (*Moshienu*), are selected from the many descriptive phrases and names used of God. They are perhaps those most frequently used and certainly are those which tradition has invested with most significance. The average worshiper, either from his own study of the talmudic and midrashic tradition or from rabbinical discourses and sermons, was thoroughly acquainted with the meanings of these various names of God; therefore, this succession of the Divine Names brought a definite connotation to his mind.

The first two names of God, *Elohenu* and *Adonenu* (*Elohim* and *Adonoy*), are always coupled in talmudic literature as related in idea. What the names meant to the writers of the Bible is a subject of scholarly dispute. Even to this day, after years of investigation, critical scholarship has not yet come to a conclusion as to the original meaning of *Elohim* and *YHVH*, the Ineffable Name of which *Adonoy* is the conventional substitute. While scholars still debate this subject, there is no question as to what meaning the teachers in the Talmud gave these two names, and, therefore, what the worshiper understood them to signify in the Prayerbook. *Elohim* is also used in the Bible to refer to judges, human judges, and, therefore, the description *Elohim* of God, means God the Judge, the stern Master of nature Whose strict justice brings punishment for evil. A medieval scholar with quaint fancy noticed that the numerical value of the Hebrew word, *Elohim* (giving the letters the number corresponding to their place in the alphabet), and the word for nature (*hateva*), amount to the same total. In a word, *Elohim* is God, the stern Judge Whose inexorable decrees, the laws of nature, punish every sin.

Balanced against this stern concept of God is the name *Adonoy*. This name associated always with its double use in Exodus (34:6), "The Lord, the Lord God, merciful and gracious," expresses God's lovingkindness, His fatherly tenderness "as a father pitieth his children." God Himself, according to the rabbis, balances these attributes of His, one against the other, sending merited punishment for evil yet forgiving iniquity and sin. The worshiper, when he uses the names *Elohim* and *Adonoy*, expresses the conviction that he deserves punishment for

· 199 ·

his misdeeds but he hopes and prays for the mercy of the Eternal Father.

The next two names of God, likewise, belong together: "God our King" and "God our Deliverer." The concept of "God the King" has long had unique connotations for the people of Israel. It was basic to the whole theory and feeling for democracy. The thought is that when God redeemed the slaves from Pharaoh's yoke He acquired them for Himself and He alone became their Master and their King. Therefore, in the song which Israel sang at the deliverance from the Red Sea, God is proclaimed as Eternal King, "The Lord shall reign for ever and ever" (Exod. 15:18). If God alone was their King no mortal king really should reign over Israel. That is why Josephus coined the phrase "theocracy," to describe the system of government in Israel. God alone was the ruler (Contra Apionem II, 17). This was understood in the Bible; when the judge Gideon was offered the position of king by the people he refused, saying, "I shall not rule over you, nor shall my children rule over you. God shall rule over you." So, too, when in the time of Samuel, the last of the judges, the people insisted upon having a mortal king, Samuel complained to God, Who said to him, "Not thee have they despised, but Me have they despised that I be not King over them."

The idea that God alone was King gave the prophets courage to speak in God's name against the mortal kings, for they were, as it were, merely lieutenants of Divinity. It explains the strong spirit of democracy that runs through all Jewish history.

The fourth epithet descriptive of God, "Deliverer," is connected with the idea of God as King. The Hebrew word *Moshia* used here of God, which can be translated "Savior" or "Deliverer," does not have the same significance as the words "Savior and Salvation" have in Christianity. It does not refer to a miraculous deliverance from inherited sin, although, indeed, God is looked upon as our source of forgiveness and atonement. The phrase primarily means God as Deliverer from all misfortune. Just as among other people the human king was looked upon as father and protector of his people, so God, being King, is Protector and Savior of His children. In the Book of Judges whenever Israel was subjugated by oppressors the chronicler reports, "And the Lord raised up a saviour to the children of Israel," referring to the hero judge whom God sent (Judges 3:9, 3:15, etc.). In Isaiah (43:11, 45:21), and in Hosea (13:4), the concept broadens, "There is no Deliverer beside Me." When, therefore, the authors of the Prayerbook insist that in every complete benediction the phrase to be used is not "King of Israel" but "King of the World," *Melech ho-olom*, they mean that God will bring His deliverance to all mankind.

Thus the four words describing God indicate the God-conception dear to the hearts of the people: *Elohim*, God is the Stern Judge, punishing evil, injustice, and oppression; *Adonoy*, God is merciful, forgiving, and tender; *Melech*, God alone is King, and democracy is Israel's ideal; *Moshia*, God will deliver all men from grief and tragedy.

These four descriptions of God are repeated in every stanza of the poem, each time with a different introduction. According to the earlier sources what is now the second verse, "Who is like our God, etc.," was originally the first verse. This seems logical. The hymn, then, begins with a question, "Who is like our God, etc.?" then would come the second stanza as an answer, *Ein Kelohenu*, "There is no one like our God, etc." This question and answer express a technique used in many biblical texts. Among the earliest passages in biblical literature is the song that Israel sang as it crossed the Red Sea. In this song the question is asked (Exod. 15:11), "Who is like Thee, O Lord, among the mighty?" The entire poem, *Ein Kelohenu*, may, indeed, be considered as a sort of a metric commentary to this famous verse which has a prominent place in the daily service in the blessing following the Sh'ma Yisroel. The same question reappears often in Scripture, as for example, Psalm 71:19, "O God, who is like unto Thee?" The answer of the second stanza is also based on a scriptural text. Thus, I Samuel 2:2, "There is none holy as the Lord; for there is none besides Thee; neither is there any rock like our God." A similar idea is expressed in II Samuel 7:22, "There is none like Thee, neither is there any God besides Thee." Thus, question and answer express the thought common in Jewish literature that God is unique, God is incomparable.

The third stanza reads, "Let us give thanks to our God, to our Lord, etc." In other words, if there is none like unto Him then let us not waste our devotion on unworthy objects, let our thanks go to Him alone. In response to this invocation comes the last stanza, "Praised be our King, praised be our God, etc."

Just when and why the first two stanzas became interchanged, the answer, "There is none," coming before the question, "Who is there like," we do not know; but Rashi, the great biblical commentator of the twelfth century, already knew the hymn in its present form with the answer before the question. He calls attention to an interesting acrostic which the stanzas make.

Ein (there is none), *Mi* (who is like), and *Node* (let us thank), form the word Amen; the fourth stanza, "Praised be He," is the standard beginning of a blessing. Thus, we have the phrase, "Amen, Praised be He," expressing man's attitude to the Judge and Father, King and Deliverer, namely: whatever He in His providence sends us, to that we say Amen, Praised be He.

B. Adon Olom. The widely popular hymn, *Adon Olom*, is, like *Ein Kelohenu*, of unknown authorship. Although, because of its poetic beauty, it has been ascribed to the great medieval poet, Solomon ibn Gabirol, yet it is known to be much older and in all likelihood dates back to the g'onic period. This hymn is recited in some rituals at the beginning of the daily Morning Service, by others also at the close of the Sabbath Eve Service, and by many pious people at night before retiring.

The literary style of *Adon Olom* is strikingly different from that of *Ein Kelohenu*. The *Ein Kelohenu* is a simple repetition of almost identical lines whereas the successive stanzas of *Adon Olom* express a rich variety of thought and imagery. In fact, *Adon Olom* is a perfect example of medieval Hebrew poetry at its best: an exact rhythm and rhyme scheme, a brilliant expression of profound thought in simple, beautiful, and memorable diction.

Like *Ein Kelohenu*, its theme is God, His nature, and our relations to Him. But whereas in
Ein Kelohenu, the various concepts of God come
as connotations of the various names of God used
in every stanza, here the nature of God is ex-
pressly described. The following translation by
Israel Zangwill follows the Hebrew closely:

> Lord of all the world, He reigned alone
> While yet the universe was naught
> When by His will all things were wrought,
> Then first his sovran name was known.
>
> And when the All shall cease to be,
> In dread lone splendour He shall reign.
> He was, He is, He shall remain
> In glorious eternity.
>
> For He is one, no second shares
> His nature or His holiness;
> Unending and beginningless
> All strength is His, all ways He bears.
>
> He is the living God to save,
> My Rock while sorrows toils endure
> My banner and my stronghold sure,
> The cup of life whene'er I crave.
>
> I place my soul within His palm
> Before I sleep as when I wake,
> And though my body I forsake,
> Rest in the Lord in fearless calm.

The first two stanzas describe in poetic language the deeper meaning of God's eternity. The

concept of God's eternity is a difficult one particularly since time itself was looked upon as a creation of God. We live in time, all our thoughts are limited by time and we naturally, therefore, think in terms of beginning and end. The poet asserts that before the creation of the world, therefore before time itself was created, God existed, and after the world will cease to exist God, the Timeless, will endure forever (see Kohler, *Jewish Theology*, page 98). This idea, that God the Creator of the world, preceded the world and will outlast it, is found frequently in biblical literature. The very concept underlying the story of Creation involves this idea. Before the Creation God hovered over the chaos; and the psalmist adds the other half of this idea, Psalm 102:26-28:

> Of old Thou didst lay the foundation of the earth;
> And the heavens are the work of Thy hands.
> They shall perish, but Thou shalt endure;
> Yea, all of them shall wax old like a garment;
> As a vesture shalt Thou change them, and they shall pass away;
> But Thou art the selfsame,
> And Thy years shall have no end.

The thought is frequently expressed in the latter part of the Prophet Isaiah (44:6):

> Thus saith the Lord, the King of Israel,
> And his Redeemer the Lord of hosts:

> I am the first, and I am the last,
> And beside Me there is no God.

(See also Isa. 41:4, 48:12.)

This quality of eternity is not only an attribute of God, it is the attribute of God alone. Aristotle, who exerted so weighty an influence, particularly in the Middle Ages, asserted that not only was God eternal but matter, too, was eternal. He could not conceive of a time when the material of the universe did not exist. But to the Jew the concept of eternity, of timelessness, pertains to God alone. Hence the third stanza that God is One and none can compare unto Him. The "One" here means God is unique, the only One Who is Eternal.

This concept of God, eternal above time, would tend to make God so transcendent as to be beyond reach of human prayers and devotion. Hence the hymn continues in the fourth stanza, with the assertion that although God is Eternal and transcendent, He yet is near enough to man to guard and deliver him in time of trouble. God is not only transcendent; he is also immanent in every heart and in every human destiny. This combination of opposites is frequently found in Jewish theology. Whether these opposites can be logically harmonized or not, they are a psychological necessity for true religion. Thus God is the Stern Judge (*Elohim*)

Who through His strict natural law punishes all sin, yet He is also the loving Father Who tenderly forgives and protects. Thus, too, God is omniscient. He foresees every human action beforehand, yet He gives man free will to choose between good and evil. Judaism has long understood that a true and effective religion requires both of these opposites, and has left it to the philosophers to find a method of harmonizing them.

The last stanza speaks of God as our living Redeemer. The phrase is taken from Job, who in the midst of his personal tragedies, says (19: 25), "I know that my Redeemer liveth." The phrase, "the cup of life," is taken from Psalm 16:5 in which God is described, "O Lord, the portion of mine inheritance and of my cup, Thou maintainest my lot." The last sentence of the *Adon Olom*, "I place my soul within His palm both when I sleep and when I wake," is based upon the well-known idea that in sleep the soul leaves the body and may or may not return. Sleep is a foretaste of death. Therefore, it is in God's hands that we place our spirit when we sleep. Hence, in the night prayers we say, "Lighten my eyes, lest I sleep the sleep of death," Psalm 13:4. And also the phrase, "Into Thy hand I commit my spirit, Thou hast redeemed me, O Lord, Thou God of truth," Psalm 31:6.

The closing phrase, "The Lord is for me; I will not fear," is taken from Psalm 118:6.

This closing stanza, that the worshiper commit his soul into God's hands whether he is asleep or awake, is generally taken as a proof that this beautiful hymn was originally written as a night prayer. As a matter of fact, it is included among the night prayers; but whether it was originally a night prayer or not, it fits into the Morning Service where it is usually found and in any other service, too, because it expresses the profound trust of the worshiper in God. The very greatness of God, His transcendence over all time, His preexistence, and His endurance after the world shall pass away, does not for the Jewish worshiper make Him less intimate and accessible. He is still the Rock, the Banner, the Cup of Salvation, the Guardian at every hour and in all circumstances of life.

C. *Yigdal*. The hymn *Yigdal* is one of the most popular hymns in the liturgy. It is found in the Morning Service and also in the Evening Service and like *Adon Olom* and *Ein Kelohenu* has many musical settings. The authorship of this poem is likewise not quite certain. However, there is a general agreement that it was written in Italy in the fourteenth century. The translation by Israel Zangwill follows the Hebrew closely:

1. The living God O magnify and bless,
   Transcending Time and here eternally.
2. One Being, yet unique in unity;
   A mystery of Oneness and measureless.
3. Lo! form or body He has none, and man
   No semblance of His holiness can frame.
4. Before Creation's dawn He was the same;
   The first to be, though never He began.
5. He is the world's and every creature's Lord;
   His rule and majesty are manifest,
6. And through His chosen, glorious sons ex-
   prest
   In prophecies that through their lips are
   poured.
7. Yet never like to Moses rose a seer,
   Permitted glimpse behind the veil divine.
8. This faithful prince of God's prophetic line
   Received the Law of Truth for Israel's ear.
9. The Law God gave He never will amend,
   Nor ever by another Law replace.
10. Our secret things are spread before His face;
    In all beginnings He beholds the end.
11. The saint's reward He measures to his meed;
    The sinner repays the harvest of his ways.
12. Messiah He will send at end of days,
    And all the faithful to salvation lead.
13. God will the dead again to life restore
    In His abundance of Almighty love.

This philosophic poem, like the *Adon Olom*, gives in clear detail the theologian's concept of the nature of God and His relationship to man. It is, in fact, a poetic version of the thirteen articles, the creed of the great philosopher Maimonides. It must be understood that Judaism never has had an official creed in the sense that Christianity has, namely, an official list of the articles of faith drawn up by an official ecclesiastical body, compulsory for every adherent of the faith. In fact, Maimonides' thirteen articles were disputed by many of his contemporaries and successors, and other philosophers have drawn up other statements of belief containing three or four or other enumerations of articles (see "Articles of Faith," *Jewish Encyclopedia*, II, 148 ff.). However, the articles of Maimonides, owing to the clear, succinct language in which they were composed, and the high authority and standing of their author, were widely read and appear in prose form in many prayerbooks, not, however, as a compulsory part of the ritual. They are found in the Prayerbook following the Morning Service and are for voluntary reading. These thirteen articles have appealed to many poets as an appropriate theme; at least forty poetic versions of Maimonides' Creed are extant in Jewish literature. But of all these the poem *Yigdal* became the one universally accepted and embodied in the Prayerbook. It follows the creed closely, dealing with the articles in succession: first, a belief in the existence of a Creator; second, belief in the resurrection of the dead (see *A Companion to the Daily Prayerbook* by Singer and Abrahams, page 103). In the Reform Prayerbook the last article is reworded to express the belief in spiritual immortality rather than bodily resurrection.

D. L'cho Dodi. The latest of all hymns to have been accepted into all the rituals is the poem, "The Sabbath Bride," written by Solomon al kabetz Halevi, who lived in the city of Safed, Palestine, in the sixteenth century (see also Chapter xi). This hymn bears the acrostic of the author's name, Solomon Halevi, indicated by the opening letters of each stanza. The hymn is difficult to translate because it is constructed of brilliantly combined fragments of verses chiefly from Isaiah and these fragments worked together into an artistic mosaic. A literal translation of the fourth, fifth, and sixth stanzas, followed by the biblical source of each phrase will indicate with what skill the poet selected fragments of Scripture and wove them together into one beautiful unity.

> Shake thyself from the dust, (Isa. 52:2)
> Put on thy beautiful garments, (Isa. 52:1) O my people,
> Through the son of Jesse of Bethlehem, Draw nigh unto my soul, and redeem it; (Psalm 69:19)
>
> Awake, awake, (Isa. 51:17)
> Arise, shine, for thy light is come, (Isa. 60:1)
> Awake, awake, utter a song, (Judges 5:12)
> The glory of the Lord is risen upon thee (Isa. 60:1).

Thou wilt not be ashamed nor disgraced, (Isa. 54:4)
Then why art thou cast down, why dost thou moan, (Psalm 42:12)
And in her shall the afflicted of His people take refuge, (Isa. 14:32)
And the city shall be builded upon her own mound (Jer. 30:18).

Thus the poem rings with biblical echoes, combining the familiar with the new, harmonizing past and present. An acceptable poetic translation is found in the *Standard Book of Jewish Verse* (page 265):

Come forth, my friend, the bride to meet,
Come, O my friend, the Sabbath greet.

"Observe ye" and "remember" still
The Sabbath—thus His Holy will
God in one utterance did proclaim.
The Lord is One, and One His name
To Him renown and praise and fame.
   Come forth, my friend, the bride to meet,
   Come, O my friend, the Sabbath greet.

Greet we the Sabbath at our door,
Well-spring of blessing evermore
With everlasting gladness fraught,
Of old ordained, divinely taught,
Last in creation, first in thought,
   Come forth, my friend, the bride to meet,
   Come, O my friend, the Sabbath greet.

Arouse thyself, awake and shine,
For lo! it comes, the light divine;
Give forth a song and over thee

The glory of the Lord shall be
Revealed in beauty speedily.
  Come forth, my friend, the bride to meet,
  Come, O my friend, the Sabbath greet.

Crown of thy husband come in peace.
Come, bidding toil and trouble cease.
With joy and cheerfulness abide
Among thy people true and tried,
Thy faithful people—come O bride,
  Come forth, my friend, the bride to meet,
  Come, O my friend, the Sabbath greet.

See also the version based upon the above in the *Union Prayerbook*, page 26.

The theme of the poem is derived mainly from a statement in the Talmud (b. Shabos 119a) that Rabbi Hanina dressed himself in his best clothes on Friday evening and said, "Come let us go forth to meet the Sabbath Queen." Rabbi Yannai also greeted the Sabbath with the words, "Come, O Bride; come, O Bride." The ceremony observed by these rabbis may have represented some local custom or may have been the expression of their personal joy at the coming of the Sabbath. But it was not till twelve centuries later that we first encounter a regular liturgical custom to greet the Sabbath bride. In the sixteenth century, in the great center of mysticism founded in the city of Safed, Palestine, chiefly by exiles or descendants of exiles from Spain, the custom arose actually to march out on Friday evening to greet the Sabbath. These processions to greet the Sabbath bride or queen were accompanied by the chanting of Psalms, "Come let us sing to the Lord," "Sing to the Lord a new song," (Psalms 95-99, and 29). (See above, Chapter xi.)

The poet of this group of Palestinian mystics was Solomon al kabetz Halevi and the poem that he wrote was composed for these processions. This explains why the poem is written as a march, "Come to greet the bride, etc.," or "Let us go forth to meet the Sabbath." As a reminiscence of the original use of the hymn, many congregations retain the custom of turning toward the door as the words of the last stanza are repeated, "Come O Bride; come O Bride."

The whole poem breathes a joy and a tenderness which many ill-informed writers believe alien to the Jewish religion. A loving joy in greeting the Sabbath contradicts the bitter, gloomy picture of Judaism painted by prejudiced theologians. This mood of happiness is not merely the product of the enthusiastic mystic school of Safed. It goes back as we see to the Talmud where the Sabbath was greeted as bride, if, perhaps, only by an individual rabbi and his entourage; yet the ceremony was considered worthy of preservation by the Talmud since it evidently expressed an authentic Jewish mood. It goes even further back to the latter part of the

Book of Isaiah whence the author of the poem drew most of his phrases. There, too, Israel is described by God as His beloved wife who will be comforted and blessed with the love of her Royal Husband. (Cf. also Yalkut Shimoni to Isaiah, No. 506: "In ten places in Scripture Israel is called 'bride.'") That this late poem should have been accepted universally in Jewish liturgy all over the world is evidence enough of the true mood of the Sabbath, a mood of joy, peace, and the happiness of love.

XVI

How Precious Thy Thoughts

GEMS FROM THE PRAYERBOOK

THE greatest literary influence on the development of the Jewish Prayerbook was, of course, the Bible. The reading of the Five Books of Moses (the Torah) and the reading of the Prophets (the Haftoro) was, perhaps, as has been stated, the original occasion for the gathering of the people in regular assemblies. The singing of Temple Psalms and the reciting of non-Temple Psalms gave the synagogue its spiritual mood and its devotional content. To this day the bulk of the service consists of Law, Prophets, and Psalms.

The Bible (the Law, Prophets, and particularly the Psalms), is so rich in devotional material that it is almost sufficient in itself for any prayerbook. If the synagogue had not created any original writing and had used only the biblical material it would have found in these ancient writings sufficient vehicles for the spiritual expression needed in prayer. Yet the regular and devoted reading and study of the great biblical passages awakened an impulse toward the creation of original prayers; particularly since it was the earnest desire of teachers and leaders that each man ask in prayer for personal needs growing out of his daily experience. Such personal petitions found simple, artless expression, but the influence of biblical literature was so powerful because of the respect in which it was held and, indeed, because of the profound spiritual power reflected in it that even original prayers clothed themselves in biblical phraseology so that most of the new prayers were virtually mosaics of biblical texts.

Yet the intense devotional spirit which awoke in Israel produced new prayer expressions and many of them, while indeed reminiscent of biblical phraseology, were truly creative and original. It is the purpose of this chapter to select from the various historic periods of prayer-writing those original phrases which demonstrate that the prayer-spirit in Israel was not merely the formal repetition of historic language, no matter how noble, but the living outpouring of a vital devotional spirit. Many of these phrases are found in the Talmud and were written either for private devotion or for the synagogue service. There is hardly one that does not reveal the literary soil from which it sprung but which, nevertheless, is a new flowering of idea and expression.

In the early morning prayer is the famous prayerbook phrase, "O Lord the soul which Thou hast given unto me is pure" (Singer *Prayerbook*, page 5; *Union Prayerbook*, page 101). This sentence, and the prayer of which it is a part, are given as a morning prayer in the Talmud (b. B'rochos 60b) and is a declaration that the soul of man which comes from the Divine Source is innately pure. Further on is the phrase, "As long as the soul is in me I will thank Thee God of my fathers, Lord of all creatures, Master of all souls." Likewise in the morning prayer there is the phrase, "Lord of all worlds, not in reliance upon our own righteousness do we make our supplications to Thee" (Singer *Prayerbook*, page 8; *Union Prayerbook*, page 101). This phrase is quoted in the Talmud (b. Yomo 87b) where it is given as a confession of sin for the Day of Atonement.

At the beginning of the chapters of Psalms there is the grand phrase, "Blessed be He Who spoke and the world came into being." The phrase is, of course, reminiscent of the expression in Psalm 33:9, "For He spoke, and it was; He commanded, and it stood." There are also passages in Isaiah of which this is somewhat reminiscent but whatever be the source of the thought, the phrase is terse and original. The full phrase opening this section of the service reads, "Blessed be He Who spoke and the world was; blessed be He . . . blessed be He Who speaks and acts; blessed be He Who decrees and fulfils."

In a later prayer in this same section of the service (Singer *Prayerbook*, page 33) is the famous sentence, "The Lord is King, the Lord did reign, the Lord will reign forever." This phrase, likewise, reveals biblical origins. The first part of it is related to Psalm 10:16, "The Lord is King for ever and ever"; the second to Psalm 93:1, "The Lord reigneth, He is clothed in majesty"; and the third is from Exodus (15:18), "The Lord shall reign for ever and ever." All these three scattered biblical phrases are united in this one sentence in a complete expression of the thought of God's eternity, transcending all time. This sentence became widely popular. It is used many times in the daily and holiday prayers, and many a medieval poem with complicated poetic structure used it as basis and refrain (*Union Prayerbook*, II, 352).

In the opening blessing of the section of the Sh'ma (the Yotser) there is the phrase, "Who renewest in His goodness daily and continually the works of creation" (Singer *Prayerbook*, page 46, bottom; *Union Prayerbook*, page 118). This expression is found in the Talmud in part

(b. Chagigo 12b). It seeks to express the idea that God's creation of the world was not just a far-off event which, having once occurred, was done with forever; that the world, once created, was left to run like a machine. God had not merely started the world on its course; He Himself creates it anew every day. The miracle of the universe is renewed with every dawn and sealed with every sunset. Each day is a separate and special gift of God's goodness to His creatures.

In the second blessing before the Sh'ma, the blessing of the Torah, which speaks of God's love for His children in teaching them His Law, there is found the phrase, "Lighten our eyes in Thy Law, make loyal our hearts to Thy commandments and unify our spirits to love and revere Thy Name." The idea of God's Law illuminating the eyes is based upon the verse in Proverbs (6:23): "For the commandment is a lamp and the teaching is a light." Likewise in Psalm 19:9: "The Commandment of the Lord is pure, enlightening the eye." The whole phrase echoes various biblical expressions yet as it stands it is original and vivid.

In the section of petitional prayers (the T'filo), the Sanctification (the K'dusho), which describes and elaborates the vision of Isaiah, in which the angels praise God with the words: "Holy, Holy, Holy, is the Lord of Hosts," has either the following phrase or some variant of it: "We hallow Thy name on earth as they hallow it in the highest heavens" (Singer *Prayerbook*, page 55; *Union Prayerbook*, page 126). This thought, original with the Prayerbook, is that God's praise resounds in unison from angels and men, from earth and heaven. The Bible in Isaiah speaks only of the angels praising God and of the Prophet astonished and afraid when he heard these praises and saw this vision; but the Prayerbook visualizes the humblest of men adding their song to the music of the spheres.

At the close of the T'filo and later at the end of the Kaddish where the phrase is repeated, is the famous Prayerbook sentence, "He Who maketh peace in the heavenly heights, may He make peace for us and for all of Israel. Amen" (Singer *Prayerbook*, page 66; *Union Prayerbook*, pp. 152, 153). This phrase rests upon the expression in Job (25:2), "He maketh peace in His high places." But the added phrase reveals the devotional spirit of the Prayerbook. Again, as with the passage from Isaiah used in the K'dusho, the passage in the Bible which inspired the Prayerbook phrase speaks of God's exalted grandeur high above the comprehension of man. But the Prayerbook once more unites heaven and earth, the Infinite with the finite and asks that the peace which reigns in the celestial spheres be reflected through God's grace to the life of man on earth.

Further on in the T'filo, in the special paragraph for Chanuko, the description of the remarkable victory of the Maccabees over overwhelming odds is described in these concise terms: "Thou didst fight their battle and judge their cause . . . Thou gavest the mighty into the hands of the weak, the many into the hand of the few, the wicked into the hand of the righteous and the proud into the hands of those who study Thy law." An echo of part of the phraseology here used is found in Joel (4:10), "Let the weak say: 'I am strong,'" but aside from this and a few biblical reminiscences, these sentences are all original.

In the Adoration Prayer, the Olenu (Singer *Prayerbook*, page 94; *Union Prayerbook*, page 71), there is the phrase, "To perfect the world under the kingdom of the Almighty." The verb "to perfect" (*saken*) means literally to straighten out that which is crooked. It is used in Ecclesiastes (1:15), "That which is crooked cannot be made straight." The whole expression reveals the realistic type of idealism to be found throughout the prayerbook. The world is, indeed, crooked, twisted, and perverse. It needs to be "straightened out," and it can only be straightened out with the aid of the Divine Power and man's humble acknowledgment of God's Kingship, for human self-worship leads to belligerent national pride while the acceptance of God's Sovereignty leads to human unity and the perfecting of the world. The same paragraph towards its close contains the sentence, "For Thine is the Kingdom and forever Thou wilt reign in glory." The phrase is reminiscent of Psalm 145:13: "Thy kingdom is a kingdom for all ages." But the expression, as it stands, is original. This classic prayerbook phrase was clearly in the mind of the author of the Gospel when he ended the Lord's prayer (Matt. 6:13: "For Thine is the kingdom, and the power, and the glory, for ever").

In the Evening Service in the special night prayer, the second blessing after the Sh'ma (Singer *Prayerbook*, page 135; *Union Prayerbook*, page 56) the phrase is: "Spread over us the tabernacle of Thy peace (Or Thy tabernacle of peace)." This beautiful and original phrase may be a description of the mental picture evoked perhaps by the Twenty-third Psalm where the wayfarer, fleeing from enemies and danger finds safety and shelter in the tent of God, the Host. So here after the day of toil and trouble the worshiper in his night prayer asks that God admit him into His tabernacle of peace.

In every Sabbath T'filo the fourth benediction ends with the prayer, "Our God and God of our fathers" (Singer *Prayerbook*, pp. 168-169; *Union Prayerbook*, page 22), which contains the plea, "Purify our hearts that we may serve Thee in truth." This beautiful sentence, entirely original in the Prayerbook, speaks of how difficult it is for man so full of contradictory impulses to find within himself the power to serve God truly and sincerely, and, therefore, when the Sabbath peace comes he asks that God purify his heart that the worship may be pure and sincere, "That I may serve Thee in truth."

In the Sabbath Morning Service the chapters of the Psalms are augmented by the special prayer, Nishmas. In this prayer comes the famous passage: "Though our mouths were full of song as the sea, and our tongues of exultation as the multitude of its waves, . . . though our eyes shone with light like the sun and the moon, and our hands spread forth like the eagles of heaven, . . . we would still be unable to thank thee, etc." (Singer *Prayerbook*, page 182; *Union Prayerbook*, page 216.) This vivid image has become popular in the literature of the Prayerbook and is repeated a number of times in the later hymns and poems. It is found in the Talmud (b. Taanis 6b).

In the Sabbath Afternoon Service, the intervening blessing in the T'filo opens with the phrase, "Thou art One and thy Name is One, and who is like thy people Israel, an unique nation on the earth?" (Singer *Prayerbook*, page 256; *Union Prayerbook*, page 162). The thought upon which the first part of the sentence is based comes from Zechariah (14:9): "In that day the Lord shall be One, and His Name shall be one." The second part of the phrase comes from the prayer of David in 1 Chronicles (17:21): "And who is like Thy people Israel, a nation one in the earth?" These two separate biblical phrases are here brought together. The future tense of the Prophet Zechariah's dream is changed into the present tense and the idea is expressed that as God is One, so is Israel one people. Whenever Israel reflects the spirit of God, God's unity is reflected in the comradeship of Israel.

In the T'filo of the New Year Service, in which the third introductory blessing is elaborated with a universalistic vision, the prayer for the future of humanity is climaxed by the magnificent phrase, "That they may all form a single band to do thy will with a perfect heart" (Singer *Prayerbook*, page 350; *Union Prayerbook*, II, 26). The phrase "a single band" is used in the Bible (II Samuel 2:25), of an army, and here the Prayerbook magnificently reapplies the phrase to a new use, that all of mankind become "one band" not for the sake of violence (for against whom would a united humanity do battle?) but "let them be united to do Thy Will with perfect heart."

That prayer continues with a description of the joy that will reign when mankind is at last united: "Then will the just see and rejoice . . . iniquity will close her mouth and evil will all vanish like smoke when Thou wilt remove the kingdom of arrogance from the earth." The phrase, "The righteous saw it and were glad," comes from Job (22:19); the phrase, "Iniquity stoppeth her mouth," is from Job (5:16). The phrase, "Will vanish like smoke," is based upon Psalm 37:20. All these phrases are merged here into an impressive sequence.

In the fourth blessing of the T'filo for the New Year the universalistic note is again sounded, and man's great realization of God's Kingship is expressed in this magnificent phrase, "Whatsoever hath been created may understand that thou hast created it, and whatsoever hath breath in its nostrils may say, 'The Lord God of Israel is King, and his dominion ruleth over all'" (Singer *Prayerbook*, page 353; *Union Prayerbook*, II, 58).

In the Yom Kippur Service, after the confession of sin which follows every T'filo, there is a prayer mentioned in the Talmud (b. B'rochos 17a) for the Day of Atonement. It expresses the humility of man in the presence of God in these vivid words, "O my God, before I was formed I was nothing worth, and now that I have been formed I am but as though I had not been formed. Dust am I in my life: how much more so in my death" (Singer *Prayerbook*, page 388).

* * *

The creative spirit which took biblical text and remade it into new and original sentences finds magnificent expression in the later prayer-poetry of the synagogue. A number of examples will suffice to make this abundantly evident.

The group of poems called "The Song of Unity," recited one on each day of the week and ascribed to various thirteenth century authors, takes up the thought familiar in prophetic and psalm literature that God does not necessarily ask us for material gifts such as offerings and incense, but He requires the spiritual worship of modesty and of ethical living. The classic biblical expression of this idea is of course: "Wherewith shall I come before the Lord, and bow myself before God on high? Shall I come before Him with burnt-offerings, with calves of a year old? Will the Lord be pleased with thousands of rams, with ten thousands of rivers of oil . . . it hath been told thee, O man, what is good, and what the Lord doth require of thee: only to do justly, and to love mercy and to walk humbly with thy

God" (Mic. 6:6-8). This thought expressed in the first "Song of Unity" takes the verse from Psalm 40:7, "Sacrifice and meal-offering Thou hast no delight in" and completes it with this remarkable phrase, "I will build an altar from the broken fragments of my heart," and later in the same poem, "The fragments of my spirit, these are Thy sacrifices."

In the famous prayer, Un'sane Tokef, in the additional service for the New Year (*Union Prayerbook*, II, 238) the medieval writer describes the awesome scene of God's judgment of man and His decree as to who shall live and who shall die. The solemn description closes with the famous words, "And repentance, prayer, and righteousness annul the stern decree." This idea that man's thoughts and deeds may annul the stern decree which he has, indeed, hitherto deserved, is based upon a talmudic elaboration of the verse in II Chronicles (7:14): "If My people . . . shall humble themselves, and pray, and seek My face and turn from their evil ways; then I will hear from heaven, and will forgive their sin. . . ." In the Talmud (j. Taanis II, 1[65b]), the verse is interpreted to mean that repentance and prayer and righteousness avert the decree of punishment. In another talmudic passage (j. Sanhedrin 28c), repentance and prayer are deemed to be a protection against evil dreams. This phrase, rather prosaically expressed in the Talmud, is made vivid and clear by the medieval poet and is used in a setting where its meaning is most profoundly realized.

A great depth of religious emotions is plumbed by the medieval Jewish poets in Spain, particularly by Solomon Ibn Gabirol and Jehuda Halevi. Scattered through their hundreds of religious poems written for the service are phrases of rare beauty and deep devotion. The poet Gabirol expresses the prayer that as the "true worshiper loves God with all his heart" so may he receive God's answering love:

> And as Thy name to me became
> A treasure in my heart to stand,
> So let to Thee my spirit be
> A treasure held within Thy hand.
> —Gabirol No. 10, *Jewish Classics Series*

To express the eagerness of the truly devoted worshiper to come near to the presence of God the poet says:

> The living God is my desire,
> It carries me on wings of fire,
> Body and soul to Him aspire.
> —Gabirol No. 12

The word used here for "desire" in Hebrew is used in the Bible in Genesis (3:16), and in the Song of Songs (7:11), of the love of man and woman for each other; and here the thought and the word are completely spiritualized to describe the yearning of man for God.

The other great Spanish-Jewish poet, Jehuda Halevi, constantly finds original expression for the great religious emotions. His prayers ring with biblical echoes and yet his use of biblical phraseology is always fresh and new. In a famous poem expressing his yearning for Zion while he dwelt far away in the western part of the known world (in Spain), he must have had in mind Psalm 42 in which the Levite yearns from a distance to come to the courts of God. This thought he expresses in the phrase now famous in Jewish literature (No. 1, Halevi, *Jewish Classics Series*):

"My heart is in the east, and I in the uttermost west—"

The Bible in Leviticus (25:55) says of the children of Israel, "For unto Me the children of Israel are servants." This sentence, interpreted by the rabbis (b. Kidushin 22b), is understood to mean that we are bound to God's service but *only* to God's service, that a man has no right to be a slave to another human being. The Talmud says that we are slaves to God and not slaves to slaves. This thought is poetically expressed by Jehuda Halevi, who declares that service to God is perfect freedom whereas slavery to earthly things is bitter bondage:

Servants of time—the slaves of slaves are they;
The Lord's servant, he alone is free.
Therefore when each man seeketh his portion,
"The Lord is my portion," saith my soul.

—No. 66

In Job (23:3), Job asks in his bitter complaint, "Oh that I knew where I might find Him." In answer to the question of Job, Jehuda Halevi makes this magnificent response in the opening of a poem for the last day of Sukos:

Lord, where shall I find Thee?
High and hidden is Thy place;
And where shall I not find Thee?
The world is full of Thy glory.

—No. 73

(The quotations from Solomon Ibn Gabirol are from the Zangwill edition of Gabirol's poems published by the Jewish Publication Society, the Schiff *Jewish Classics*. The quotations from Jehuda Halevi are from Nina Salaman's edition of the poems of Jehuda Halevi, also published by the Jewish Publication Society, in the Schiff *Jewish Classics*.)

*　　*　　*

The *Union Prayerbook* frequently paraphrases the translation of many of the historic prayers in order to bring their thoughts into closer harmony with modern thought. It also has a large number of original prayers as, for example, introductions to the Kaddish, prayers expressing the mood of the various festivals, etc. In many of these prayers the *Union Prayerbook* uses vivid and beautiful phraseology applying the spirit of ancient tradition to modern spiritual needs. Thus, page 10, "Grant us comfort in sorrow, strength in trial and the courage to serve Thee in all our ways"; page 20, "Thou sendest us the joys that brighten our days; from Thy hand also come the sorrows that cast their shadows over them." The prayer for peace which closes the T'filo of the evening ends with the following paraphrase: "Strengthen the bonds of friendship and fellowship among the inhabitants of all lands. Plant virtue in every soul, and may the love of Thy name hallow every home and every heart" (page 22). "Thou livest within our hearts, as Thou dost pervade the world, and we through righteousness behold Thy presence" (page 39).

In the various prayers before the Kaddish the following sentences are found (pp. 72-75): "Their deeds of lovingkindness, the true and beautiful words they spoke are treasured up as incentives to conduct by which the living honor the dead. Thou art in the setting as in the rising sun, in our bereavements as in our blessings, and Thine everlasting arms uphold us in the vicissitudes of life and in our lone journey through the valley of shadows. The Psalmist said that in his affliction he learned the law of God. Indeed, not unavailing will be our grief, if it send us back to serve and bless the living. Like the stars by day, our beloved dead are not seen with mortal eyes, but they shine on in the untroubled firmament of endless time."

The following sentences are from the prayer for Friday evening during Passover:

> This was Thy will in ancient days and it is Thy law forever. Wherever the yoke of serfdom is broken, wherever tyrants are overthrown, wherever Thy children live as free men, there is Thy word fulfilled and Thy will triumphant. To every soul comes Thy command: Be servants unto Me alone and not slaves to man.

In the intervening prayer for the T'filo of Sabbath morning (page 129), the following: "Quickened by Thy spirit, may we learn how to ennoble the things of earth by sanctifying them to Thy service." And also the following on page 132:

> O may our hearts never be so carried away by material success that we make idols of wealth, station or pleasure, and in striving after them become estranged from Thee. May every new blessing bring us nearer to Thee and make us more fervent in our devotion to Thy service, more faithful to our duties and more helpful to our fellowmen. Amen.

In the Sabbath Morning Service in the welfare

prayers after the reading of the Torah, the following paraphrase is found (page 148):

> Reward with the joy of goodness the charitable and the merciful who aid the poor, care for the sick, teach the ignorant, and extend a helping hand to those who have lost their way in the world.

In the intervening blessing of the T'filo for the three festivals, the following universal hope is expressed (page 231):

> May all persecution cease, and every trace of bondage disappear from among men, so that at last a universal feast of freedom shall be celebrated in Thy name, God of Freedom, Father of mankind. Amen.

In the *Union Prayerbook*, II, 329, in the Memorial Service for the Day of Atonement, the hope for immortality is expressed thus:

> It cannot be that Thou hast endowed us with a mighty yearning after the Infinite, with an unceasing dissatisfaction with the world, its treasures and charms, only to disappoint us at last, and to give us over to nothingness after a life of struggle, anxiety and pain. Thou hast put eternity into our hearts; Thou hast filled our souls with a longing for life beyond the grave; Thou deceivest not, Thou God of truth.

Towards the close of the Day of Atonement Service in the N'ilo, as the worshipers are about to depart for their homes, the following prayer (page 364) is voiced:

Open unto us the gates of Thy love! Enter Thou with us into our home so that it may become Thy sanctuary, and Thy spirit may abide within its walls. Then will our habitation stand firm amidst the storms of life, a refuge from evil, a bulwark against temptation.

In the entire development of Jewish prayer-literature the initial inspiration has always come from the Bible. The great scriptural monument of spiritual genius did not become the exclusive property of the learned but it diffused its light into the lives of all the children of Israel. In the great democratic institution of the synagogue the worshipers of all the post-biblical generations filled their hearts and lips with the words of Moses, the prophets, and the psalmists. Then under biblical inspiration they themselves became creative. We see that every generation in Israel from the earliest founders of the synagogue all through the ages, have sought to voice their longing for God and have succeeded in finding a way to fulfil the words of the Psalmist, "Sing unto the Lord a new song" (Psalm 96:1).

XVII

Sing a New Song

MEDIEVAL POETRY

THE Prayerbook was born in an era of spiritual enthusiasm. Many influences, as we have seen, contributed to its early development. Had not these various influences appeared at the same time, this new creation in religious life might never have taken place. The experiences of the Exile and of the Return, the rich development of Psalm poetry, the increasing study of the Law by more and more laymen, the influence of the Pharisees in transferring the regularity of the Temple ritual to the services at the various synagogue meeting-houses; all these forces had to coexist so that the Synagogue and its Prayerbook could come into being.

The coexistence of these various new tendencies naturally gave the Prayerbook and the Synagogue its tremendous initial impulse and provided it with spiritual material for much further growth. New prayers were written, and the Prayerbook continued to develop for a number of centuries after the destruction of the Temple. This was to be expected, for each of the impulses which presided at the birth of the Prayerbook, bestowed a blessing of spirituality which lasted through many generations. Yet, it would be natural to assume that after a time the initial creative prayer-impulse, composed as it was of many coordinate impulses, should lose its momentum and eventually die down. Such an outcome, judging by the precedent of all movements, spiritual, intellectual, artistic, and religious, could have been looked upon as almost inevitable. The impulse to spiritual devotion was almost surely doomed to become a mere habit, a mechanical recitation of verbal formulae.

The miracle of the Jewish Prayerbook is that this normal waning of creativity never really took place. As soon as a certain stage of progress and growth drew to its inevitable end, a new stage was almost immediately manifest. From what inner strength it came, from what deeply buried root, one can hardly tell, but the "tree of life," old and gnarled as it was, always found new power and new youth.

By the seventh century of the present era, the oldest parts of the Prayerbook were certainly a thousand years old, and in that immense period of time the basic prayers had become generally fixed, their outline and most of their wording set for all time. Yet immediately a new stage of devotional creativity began, destined to last for at least another half-millennium. The period of medieval Jewish poetry began and soon flourished with an abounding luxuriousness.

Even before the seventh century certain poetic paragraphs were inserted into the service, certain hymns for the Sabbath, and penitential prayers for fast-days. But the true synagogue poetry began with the seventh century and is associated with the names of certain poets, with a certain type of writing, and with a certain content in the poems. The term for this poetry comes from the same Greek root as our English word "poem." The poems are called piyutim or generically piyut. The writers of the piyutim, the poets, were called paitanim.

There is a general similarity among all the piyutim. First, they make use of rhyme and often of meter. They make use, also, of acrostic, either alphabetic acrostic or an acrostic of the name of the author or a combination of both. They are generally didactic, that is to say, they teach either the content of the Law involved in the holiday for which they are written, or midrashic preachments dealing with the mood of the holiday. Also, although they are inserted into various parts of the service, they are not considered obligatory, some being recited in some cities, others recited in others. They were omitted under certain circumstances or were supplanted by other poems. The style and the content of the piyutim give some indication of the circumstances under which they arose. When, in certain periods of persecution, the teachers of Israel were forbidden to instruct the people as they did in the past with regard to the laws of the various festivals, or when they were also prevented from giving their general ethical preachments, the piyut was written to take the place of either the informative or the ethical-spiritual discourses. Hence, it came about that these poems, written for the various holidays, contained the laws of the holidays or a description of the mood of the holidays or were sermons of a spiritual nature based upon midrashic material. Thus, the people sang for themselves or recited for themselves the material that would normally have been found in those public discourses prohibited by the persecutor. The piyut became the substitute for the lecture and the sermon.

The fact that the piyut employs rhyme and meter indicates that it arose when the Jews came into contact with Arabic literature, perhaps even before the conquest of eastern Asia by the Arabs. Arabic poetry differs from the old Hebrew poetry, the poetry of the Bible, in poetic method. Biblical poetry is the poetry of balanced sentences and makes no conscious use of either rhyme or meter while Arabic poetry made great use of both these devices. This, also, helps us date the origin of the piyut at about the seventh century.

It seems certain that the beginnings of the piyut are to be looked for in Palestine. The persecutions of the Palestinian Jews by the Roman Empire are well known. There is, indeed, a record of a specific decree by Justinian forbidding the teaching of the entire post-biblical legal and midrashic material. This decree, or similar decrees, may have led to concealing the discourses in the disguise of poetry. Also, it was in Palestine that Jews early came in contact with Arabic literature, specifically with its complex poetic literature, which made use of the rhyme and the meter so characteristic of the piyut. At all events, the first great masters of the piyut lived in Palestine. The first name of an individual poet (paitan) is Jose ben Jose, who lived in Palestine about 600. He was followed by Jannai, a prolific synagogue poet, who lived there about 700. The most productive of all the earlier poets was Eleazar Kalir who, scholars now agree, lived in Palestine about 750. Many of his poems are still found in our Prayerbook rituals.

After this initial impulse from Palestine, the writing of synagogue poems spread all over the

Jewish world, and there was hardly a country in which there were not some Jewish poets enriching prayer-literature by their poetic embellishments. To this day in the Orient, paitanim will write special poems for special religious occasions.

This vast literary activity, lasting for at least six centuries, brought forth such an enormous mass of synagogue poetry that the late Dr. Israel Davidson merely listing the names of these poems with only a few explanatory notes of a few lines for each, needed four large volumes for his *Thesaurus of Medieval Hebrew Poetry*. This huge thesaurus, of course, lists only those whose names have been preserved. We may safely assume that a vast mass of poems written in many scattered communities were lost and no record of them remains.

It is easy to see what effect this tremendous output of synagogue literature had upon the services. In the first place, it made the Prayerbook creative. The book was not merely a text, received from the past, to be recited as a formal duty, but it became an opportunity for literary self-expression which must have been used by thousands of men all over the world in order to pour out in literary form all their disappointments and hopes. The Prayerbook remained a living voice calling to spiritual and devotional self-expression. The piyutim also gave a vast variety to the services itself. Since the basic prayers for the various festivals were essentially alike, there could easily have been a monotony in prayer, but the piyutim, adding different prayers for Passover, Shovuos, Sukos, etc., gave marked individuality to each festival and made its special characteristics evident and impressive. Furthermore, they gave variety to the services of different regions. In each country and often in individual cities the particular historical experiences, persecutions, expulsions, found their record in the piyutim. As a result, each city felt that its prayers were not just general prayers but were the personal pleas of the worshipers to God to Whom every individual is equally precious and unique.

The third effect of this poetry was to preserve much of the growing and developing culture of each section of Jewry in the Prayerbook. Thus in Spain, where philosophy and linguistics were the subject of great intellectual activity, these themes and these methods reflected themselves in a specific type of synagogue prayer. In northern Europe (Germany, Bohemia, etc.), where the chief study was not philosophy or science but Talmud and Midrash, all the midrashic and talmudic elements were mustered in the synagogue poems. Thus, the synagogue service did not dwell in the periphery of the intellectual interests of the Jewish community, pushed aside by what might have been deemed more important studies but remained the very center of Jewish spiritual life. All the new intellectual activity of philosophy, science, Talmud, Midrash, etc., contributed to the prayer-service through the new poems.

Although piyutim were written all over the world, and each group could perhaps be distinguished from any other by certain geographical characteristics, there are two main distinguishable divisions: the German group and the Spanish group, or to use the Hebrew terms which include larger geographical entities, the Ashk'nazic and the S'fardic. The best known authors of the North European or the Ashk'nazic group, flourished in the eleventh century. They were Moses ben Kalonymus, Meshulam ben Kalonymus, and Simon ben Isaac. Their poems are still found in large numbers in the holiday services of North European rituals. The following translations taken chiefly from *The Service of the Synagogue* will make clear the nature and type of some of these poems.

In the T'filo of the Morning Service for the second day of the New Year, as introduction to the Sanctification (the K'dusho prayer found in all T'filos describing the angels praising God),

Simon ben Isaac of Mainz develops a complex poem upon the liturgical verse, "The Lord is King, the Lord was King, the Lord will reign forever." Each stanza has three lines and expresses the classic thought of the K'dusho, namely, that earth and heaven unite in the praise of God. Each of the three-line stanzas uses a third of the liturgical phrase. A few stanzas will indicate the mood of the poem:

All the Hosts of Heaven
  Speak the mighty word:
    The Lord is King
All on earth abiding
  Make the blessing heard:
    The Lord was King of yore.
These and those that soar and praise together:
    The Lord shall reign forevermore.

All the Heavens' envoys
  Signal banners raise:
    The Lord is King
All the earthly rulers
  Give their wealth of praise:
    The Lord was King of yore.
These and those acknowledge all together:
    The Lord shall reign forevermore.

All the strong, high angels
  Celebrate in song:
    The Lord is King
All that journey homeward
  Full of trust and strong:
    The Lord was King of yore.
These and those as one affirm together:
    The Lord shall reign forevermore.

All who give Him service
   Lift their voices in speech:
      The Lord is King
All made great by learning
   Heights of blessing reach:
      The Lord was King of yore.
These and those that meditate together:
      The Lord shall reign forevermore.

This fine translation by Nina Salaman succeeds in reproducing the thought, the rhyme at the end of each line, and in building up the refrain in three parts for each stanza. But it does not succeed in indicating the full technical complexity of the poem. In the original Hebrew the first words of each line, after the word "all," form the initials of Simon ben Isaac, the author of the poem; that is to say, two of each three lines are used for this acrostic. The name, therefore, appears twice. In addition, the second half of each line follows the Hebrew alphabet all the way through the poem. Not only the noun in each line, but also the verb follows the acrostic. This, of course, gives the poem a feeling of artificiality. Nevertheless, it is a brilliant technical achievement and has also a fine sense of movement.

The poem is a sufficient example of how complex the structure of these poems often was. It follows the model of an earlier poem by the great Palestinian master, Eleazar Kalir which is now found in the Morning Service for the first day of the New Year in the first blessing before the Sh'ma. Kalir's poem illustrates the use of midrashic elements in the piyutim. The poem is based upon the midrashic idea (Yalkut Shimoni to Isaiah, No. 506) that in ten different places in Scripture God lovingly calls Israel a "bride," six times through Solomon in the Song of Songs, three times through Isaiah, and once through Jeremiah; and that corresponding to these ten glorifications of Israel as a "bride," God puts on ten splendid garments, the garment of glory, the garment of strength, etc. (all based upon specific biblical phrases). The poet, therefore, describes God clad in the various garments, each representing a specific work of God in the world.

The few stanzas quoted will give the mood of this poem. The translation is by Nina Salaman.

> King with might begirded,
> Name of strength eternal
> Thine the arm of triumph, Thine the fame.
>
> King in garb of vengeance,
> On the day of vengeance,
> Striking back the foemen to their shame.
>
> .   .   .
>
> King enshrined in radiance,
> Clothed in light for vesture,
> He will bring our judgment into light.

King set round with triumph,
Strong in power and purpose,
Whilst all men are empty of all might.

    .   .   .

King who probeth action,
All within His searching—
Earth and Heaven together—He shall bring.

King and God eternal,
His eternal people
Hail Him King for ever, Holy King!

This translation renders clearly the rhyme and
the thought. But it does not indicate what would
be difficult to indicate in English, the fact that
the various stanzas follow an acrostic of the alphabet.

Very few translators are able to achieve the
almost impossible task of reproducing the difficult Hebrew acrostic into an English acrostic.
Zangwill succeeded once in a poem for the eve
of the Day of Atonement. The English is almost
an exact translation of the Hebrew. The half-
obscurity of the text in the English and the unusual words which the translator is compelled to
use, reflect exactly the same difficulty in the
original Hebrew. Precisely because the author
strove for these acrostics, he was compelled to
search all of Hebrew literature to find suitable
words. That difficulty is reflected in this remarkable translation by Israel Zangwill. It is a poem

(*Omnom Ken*) by an unknown author and is part of the penitential prayers of the eve of the Day of Atonement. It asks God to listen to the worshiper and not to the voice of the accuser. The first line follows the alphabetical acrostic. Every second line ends with the word "forgiven."

A y, 'tis thus	Evil us	hath in bond;
B y Thy grace	Guilt efface	and respond,
		"Forgiven!"

C ast scorn o'er	and abhor	th'informer's word;
D ear God, deign	this refrain	to make heard,
		"Forgiven!"

. . .

T ears, regret,	witness set	in sin's place;
U plift trust	from the dust	to Thy face—
		"Forgiven!"

V oice that sighs,	tear-filled eyes,	do not spurn;
W eigh and pause,	plead my cause,	and return
		"Forgiven!"

Y ea, off-rolled—	as foretold—	clouds impure,
Z ion's folk,	free of yoke,	O assure
		"Forgiven!"

The Spanish-Jewish scholars were distinguished by their broad knowledge of philosophy and science. Among their great contributions to Jewish culture were, first, a development of the philosophic implications of Judaism in relationship to Aristotle and Plato and the Arabic philosophy; and secondly, the development of Hebrew grammar and linguistics, thus raising the study of the text of the Bible to a true science. Both these achievements are reflected in the poetry of the Spanish-Jewish school. The poets, who based their work upon a fuller and a deeper knowledge of biblical Hebrew, did not need to search for out-of-the-way words in Bible and Midrash as did the northern paitanim and, therefore, their poetry is simpler and clearer. Through this simplicity the poet often expresses a profound philosophic and spiritual idea. Very few of these magnificent poems have found their way into the Prayerbooks of northern Europe but those that have are particularly significant.

There is a poem used at the beginning of the Morning Service by the great master of Spanish poetry, Solomon Ibn Gabirol. This short four-stanza poem in clear, simple style, carries the four letter acrostic of the author's name, Solomon. It is a morning prayer, an introduction to the service. In this brief poem the author deals with the theological problem of how may we presume to pray to God since God is omniscient and knows our thoughts even before we utter them. To which question the philosopher-poet answers that our prayers are not for the purpose of informing God but because God in His fatherly love desires to hear the voice of His children. The translation given is by Alice Lucas.

MORNING SONG

At the dawn, I seek Thee,
  Refuge and rock sublime,—
Set my prayer before Thee in the morning,
  And my prayer at eventime.

I before Thy greatness
  Stand, and am afraid:—
All my secret thoughts Thine eye beholdeth
  Deep within my bosom laid.

And withal what is it
  Heart and tongue can do?
What is this my strength, and what is even
  This the spirit in me too?

But verily man's singing
  May seem good to Thee;
So will I thank Thee, praising, while there
    dwelleth
  Yet the breath of God in me.

A penitential poem (*Shikchi Y'gonech*) by Gabirol is used in the *Union Prayerbook* (II, 330). The version is based upon a translation by Alice Lucas. It describes the storm-tossed soul of man, worn down with grief and worry and adjures man not to be too concerned with transient life but to pray for forgiveness and union with God. The poem contains the acrostic of the author's name.

O soul, with storms beset,
Thy griefs and cares forget!
Why dread earth's transient woe,
When soon thy body in the grave unseen
Shall be laid low,
And all will be forgotten then, as though
It had not been?

Why muse, O troubled soul,
O'er life's poor earthly goal?
When thou hast fled, the clay
Lies mute, nor bear'st thou aught of wealth, or
    might
With thee that day,
But, like a bird, unto thy nest away,
Thou wilt take flight.

Life is a vine, whose crown
The reaper Death cuts down.
His ever-watchful eyes
Mark every step, until night's shadows fall,
And swiftly flies
The passing day, and ah! how distant lies
The goal of all.

Before God's mercy-seat
His pardoning love entreat.
Make pure thy thoughts from sin,
And bring a contrite heart as sacrifice
His grace to win—
Then will His angels come and lead thee in
To Paradise.

The other great master of Spanish-Jewish poetry, Jehuda Halevi, wrote thousands of poems
which found their way into various rituals as far
east as India. Yet very few of his poems are found

in the rituals of northern Europe. One poem of his in our ritual is for the seventh day of Passover. According to tradition the seventh day of Passover was the day when Israel successfully crossed the divided Red Sea and the Egyptian host, pursuing them, were drowned in the returning waters. On this theme, Jehuda Halevi wrote a poem. This poem is appropriately placed in the service, having been written for the blessing following the Sh'ma, which always deals with the redemption from Egypt. This prayer always ends with the seal, "Praised be Thou, O Lord, Who hast redeemed Israel." Hence, all poems by medieval poets, inserted at this point, are classified as Redemption Poems (*G'ulo*). This poem by Jehuda Halevi, for the seventh day of Passover, the anniversary of the crossing of the Red Sea, carries the acrostic of the author's name. The translation is by Nina Salaman.

> The day the saved of God
> Traversed the deep dryshod,
>> *Then a new song*
>> *Sang Thy redeemed throng.*
>
> Lo, sunken in deceit
> The Egyptian daughter's feet,
> But lo, the Shulamite (i.e., Israel)
> Went shod in fair delight.
>> *Then a new song*
>> *Sang Thy redeemed throng.*

. . .

Here the author, following the thought of the blessing in which this poem is inserted, turns from the redemption from Egypt in the past to a prayer that God redeem those who are now oppressed.

> Thy banners Thou wilt set
> O'er those remaining yet,
> And gather those forlorn
> As gathering ears of corn.
> > *Then a new song*
> > *Sang Thy redeemed throng.*
>
> Ah, take her as of yore,
> And cast her forth no more
> Let sunlight crown her day
> And shadows flee away.
> > *Then a new song*
> > *Sang Thy redeemed throng.*

A New Year poem by Jehuda Halevi for the Morning Service expresses the mood of union with God, the desire to serve God alone (*Mi Yitneni*, No. 126, Brody Divan). The poem carries an acrostic of the author's name. The translation is by Israel Zangwill (*Standard Book of Jewish Verse*, page 436).

SERVANT OF GOD

O would that I might be
A servant unto Thee,
Thou God of all adored!
Then, though by friends outcast,
Thy hand would hold me fast,
And draw me near to Thee, my King and Lord.

Spirit and flesh are Thine,
O Heavenly Shepherd mine;
My hopes, my thoughts, my fears, Thou seest all,
Thou measurest my path, my steps dost know
When Thou upholdest, who can make me fall?
When Thou restrainest, who can bid me go?
O would that I might be
A servant unto Thee,
Thou God by all adored.
Then, though by friends outcast,
Thy hand would hold me fast,
And draw me near to Thee, my King and Lord.

Fain would my heart come nigh
To Thee, O God on high,
But evil thoughts have led me far astray
From the pure path of righteous government,
Guide Thou me back into Thy holy way,
And count me as one impenitent.
O would that I might be
A servant unto Thee,
Thou God, by all adored!
Then, though by friends outcast,
Thy hand would hold me fast,
And draw me near to Thee, my King and Lord.

So lead me that I may
Thy Sovereign will obey;
Make pure my heart to seek Thy truth divine,
When burns my wound, be Thou with healing near!
Answer me, Lord! for sore distress is mine,
And say unto Thy servant, I am here.
O would that I might be
A servant unto Thee,
Thou God, by all adored!
Then, though by friends outcast,
Thy hand would hold me fast,
And draw me near to Thee, my King and Lord.

These few examples are sufficient to indicate the mood and the extent of this great branch of Jewish prayer literature. Aside from the spiritual nature of the poems the cultural scope which they cover is in itself remarkable. They reveal a thorough knowledge, not only of every corner of biblical literature but of the whole mass of talmudic and midrashic writings. When we reflect how popular these poems were, we realize that they were written not merely for learned men but for a public whose mass learning was unique in all the history of culture. Of course, in later years the poems were perhaps no longer clearly understood by the average readers, yet the fact that they had become so vastly popular in the period when they were written, indicates obviously that the average Jew must have understood them and was at home in vast reaches of the traditional literature. They were written by remarkable men for an extraordinary public.

Perhaps more important than the cultural implication of the development of this literature is its spiritual implication. That the Prayerbook should have been so enlarged and amplified and should have attracted all this literary creativity, indicates that the devotional spirit, which so many centuries before, had given to the world its first regular purely spiritual worship of God, had never lost its creative power.

· XVIII ·

When Thou Sittest in Thy House

HOME PRAYERS

SCHECHTER (in the second series of the *Stud-ies in Judaism*, page 70) makes the follow-ing comment with regard to the relation-ship of temple, synagogue, and home in Israel in the time of Ben Sira:

> The Synagogue found a powerful auxiliary in the home. The Sabbath was then more strictly observed than in later ages. The dietary laws, forming a part of the holiness code, and probably kept originally only by the priests, now helped to hallow every Jewish home which came under the influence of the synagogue. . . . These tended to give distinction and character to the nation at large. The Synagogue became a Tem-ple on a small scale, and the Jewish home a Syn-agogue in miniature.

The general democratic tendency in the time of the Second Temple, culminating in the activi-ties of the Pharisees, helped to augment the in-fluence of the Synagogue by diminishing the influence of the Sadducean priestly families who controlled the Temple on Mount Zion. That same democratic tendency was carried further beyond the synagogue into every household. Not only was sanctity transferred from the one central sanctuary to the scattered synagogues all over the land, but beyond the synagogue into the home. More and more of the observances of the priests in the Temple found their reflection in the homes of Israel. Schechter speaks of the dietary laws which probably were first observed only by the priests since they were to be specially holy owing to their sacerdotal function. These dietary laws were made the privilege and the obligation of the average man since each man was part of "a kingdom of priests."

The general development of home ritual reveals many phases of the same tendency. On the Sabbath and festivals the home meal was introduced by a wine service of sanctification (Kiddush) which was obviously related to the wine libation in the Temple. On the table whole loaves of bread were displayed and blessed, a custom recalling the shewbread in the Temple. The meal began and ended with prayer, the whole ritual tending to express the idea that the home was a sanctuary, the table an altar, and the parent a priest. The full spirit of Jewish worship is not complete unless a study be made of worship in the home, the inner sanctuary of Israel.

The chief ritual in the home was the ceremonial meal on the Sabbath. This, occurring every week, brought a regular accession of holiness into the home. The service begins by the lighting of candles by the mother. While Jewish literature connects this ceremony of lighting the candles with the light of creation inasmuch as the Sabbath commemorates the climax of the six days of God's Creation of the world, it brings to mind, likewise, the solemn lighting of the menorah in front of the curtain before the Holy of Holies by the priest. The table is set with a special table-cloth, and an additional cloth is placed over the two loaves of bread, which represent the double portion of manna given to Israel in the desert on the Sabbath day (Exod. 16:5). Although these loaves of bread are connected with the manna in the wilderness, they are clearly reminiscent of the loaves of shewbread in the Temple, as mentioned above.

The Sabbath meal itself begins with the Kiddush, a ritual over the wine. This service over the wine is connected by the rabbis with the verse (Exod. 20:8), "Remember the Sabbath day," which they interpreted to mean remember to speak of the Sabbath over the wine. But it is definitely connected with the wine libation in the Temple. The Kiddush, the sanctification of the day, over the wine for the Sabbath and the festivals, is related in text and thought with the fourth and intervening blessing of the T'filo on Sabbath and holidays. This blessing is, likewise, called "the sanctification of the day" (K'dushas Hayom). The rabbis recognized that this prayer in the synagogue and the wine at the table were for the same purpose, and they discussed which of the two sanctifications was the more important. The text of the wine ceremony (the Kiddush), like the text of the blessing in the T'filo, speaks of God "Who hast sanctified us with His commandments, given us the Sabbath in love and in favour." The institution of the wine ceremony is old. It is discussed before the beginning of the present era by the disciples of Hillel and Shammai (m. B'rochos VIII, 1). In fact, the rabbinical theory is that the Kiddush was ordained by "the men of the Great Synagogue," the followers of Ezra, in the fifth pre-Christian century (b. B'rochos 33a).

At the close of the meal there is the grace after meals. The practice of reciting grace after meals is based upon the biblical verse (Deut. 8:10), "And thou shalt eat and be satisfied, and bless the Lord thy God for the good land which He hath given thee." The original form of the grace after meals consisted of three blessings, thanks to God as the provider of food and sustenance: "Blessed art thou . . . who feedest the whole world with thy goodness, . . . thou givest food to all flesh, for thy lovingkindness endureth for ever . . . providest food for all thy creatures whom thou hast created. Blessed art thou, O Lord, who givest food unto all" (Singer *Prayerbook*, page 425). The second blessing thanks God for having redeemed Israel from Egypt and taught Israel the Law, and ends up again with a blessing and thanks for food. Its seal, therefore, is, "Praised be Thou, O Lord, for the land and for the food." Then the third blessing, which speaks of Jerusalem, contains the words, "O God our Father, feed us, nourish us, grant us relief from all our troubles," and ends, "Praised be Thou Who in Thy compassion re-buildest Jerusalem." According to the Talmud, a fourth blessing speaking of God, the Good and the Beneficent, "Who shall be praised through-out all generations," was added after the de-struction of Jerusalem (b. B'rochos 48b).

The logical sequence of these blessings is note-worthy. The first thought of the Israelite thank-ing God daily for his food, is not for himself as a child of Israel but for all the children of God Who feeds and sustains all His creatures. Only after clear emphasis has been made that God is universal does the worshiper speak definitely of God's special goodness to the people of Israel for having delivered them from Egypt and taught them His Law; then, more specifically, a prayer for Jerusalem and the sanctuary, and a prayer for redemption. This is similar to the sequence of thought in the successive T'filos of the Sabbath (see Chapter xi). This succession of ideas, God the Universal Creator and Provider, God the Guide of history and Teacher, God the Protector and the Redeemer, is an essential religious attitude in Judaism, for it runs through many of the services in synagogue and home.

The Kiddush, by which the sanctification of the Sabbath or holiday is proclaimed at the meal in the home, is also recited in the synagogue at the close of the service ushering in the sacred day. The explanation given for the presence of this home ceremonial in the synagogue service is that the strangers were entertained in the synagogue and thus it became their home (see Chapter xi).

As the Sabbath and the holidays were ushered in by a sanctification, a Kiddush, so they were ushered out by a special home ceremonial, a separation (a *Havdolo*). The *Havdolo* is a more elaborate ceremony than the Kiddush; it contains four elements in place of the two elements in the Kiddush. In the Kiddush there is the wine ceremony and the prayer of sanctification cited above. In the *Havdolo*, there is also the wine and in place of the prayer of sanctification the prayer of separation of the sacred from the profane. In addition to these two, the *Havdolo* has a blessing over fire and light and a blessing over the spices. The blessing over the spices (*b'somim*) is generally explained as a refreshment of the spirit to strengthen it after the departure of the "extra-soul" with which man is imbued on the Sabbath. The blessing over the light and fire is derived from the idea that since on the Sabbath no fire may be lighted, the beginning of the week of work is signalized by the fact that now we may use fire, hence the blessing. In the *Havdolo* ceremony a twisted candle of many wicks is used instead of a single candle as on Friday evening. The reason given for this is that in the text of the blessing "Praised be Thou . . . Who createst the lights of fire" the plural "lights" is used. The blessing of separation corresponds to the blessing of sanctification at the beginning of a festival. It reads: "Blessed art thou . . . who makest a distinction between holy and profane, between light and darkness . . . between the seventh day and the six working days. Blessed art thou, O Lord, who makest a distinction between holy and profane" (Singer *Prayerbook*, pp. 310-311).

The most dramatic of all the home services is the service for the eve of Passover. This home service is more elaborate than the festival service in the synagogue. Passover was a home service before it became a public service. The description in Exodus (12:1 ff.) of the observance of the festival describes a home festival, the lamb slaughtered by every household, the blood sprinkled on the doorposts, meat eaten by the family. Gradually, of course, it became a public festival. The law required that Passover (like Shovuos and Sukos) be a pilgrimage festival. The men had to come to Jerusalem to celebrate the festival there. How Passover was celebrated in the days of the Second Temple by those who did not go to Jerusalem is not clear but an elaborate home ritual developed. The older sources (*Mishnah P'sochim*) describes the ritual of preparing the house for Passover and the last chapter of the Tractate P'sochim describes the Seder. The essence of the home service is the narrative of the Exodus which is told in great elaboration, in fact, it is considered praiseworthy to tell the story at length and in detail. Four cups of wine are drunk, said to correspond to the four terms for redemption used in the Exodus story (Exod. 6:6). The story of the redemption is told in answer to questions asked by a child. The various symbols of the Passover are demonstrated and described. The Hallel Psalms (Psalms 113-118) are chanted, partly before the meal and partly after the meal with the grace after the meal. This entire home service is printed in a separate book-let, the narrative of Passover (*Haggadah Shel Pesach*).

Another significant home ritual is the observance of Chanuko. The lights are kindled in the home and the blessing recited over them. And in later times the famous hymn, *Mooz Tsur*, became part of the service. For a modern version of this hymn (Rock of Ages) see *Union Prayer-book*, page 92.

Just as the regular prayers were augmented in the Middle Ages by medieval poetry so the home services, likewise, received the same elaboration. The Friday evening home ritual, particularly, is enriched by table songs (*z'miros*). One of the best known is ascribed to Isaac Luria, the great leader of the mystic school of the city of Safed in the sixteenth century (see Chapter XI). The poem expresses the spirit of serene joy, the central mood of the Sabbath. The translation is by Nina Davis.

> *This day is for Israel light and rejoicing,*
> *A Sabbath of rest.*
> Thou badest us standing assembled at Sinai
>   That all the years through we should keep thy
>   behest—
> To set out a table full-laden, to honor
>   The Sabbath of rest.
> *This day is for Israel light and rejoicing*
>   *A Sabbath of rest.*

Treasure of heart for the broken people,
  Gift of new soul for the souls distrest,
Soother of sighs for the prisoned spirit—
  The Sabbath of rest.
This day is for Israel light and rejoicing
  A Sabbath of rest.

When the work of the worlds in their wonder
    was finished,
  Thou madest this day to be holy and blest,
And those heavy-laden found safety and stillness,
  A Sabbath of rest.
This day is for Israel light and rejoicing,
  A Sabbath of rest.

Many table hymns of this type, some in Hebrew and some in Aramaic, became popular and were sung in almost every household.

In addition to all these family observances in the home, the home was a house of prayer in the sense that particularly on week-days when many men could not go to the synagogue they recited the regular daily prayers in the home. The home was considered sacred enough for this purpose and a prayer offered at home was acceptable to God. In addition, early morning prayers and night prayers are recited in the home. The night prayer, of course, includes the Sh'ma Yisroel, which originally was recited on retiring and also contains the blessing which expresses the familiar thought that sleep is akin to death, that we put our soul in God's Hands and ask Him to restore life to us in the morning.

Blessed art thou, O Lord our God, King of the universe, who makest the bands of sleep to fall upon mine eyes, and slumber upon mine eyelids. May it be thy will, O Lord my God and God of my fathers, to suffer me to lie down in peace and to let me rise up again in peace. . . . O lighten mine eyes, lest I sleep the sleep of death, for it is thou who givest light to the apple of the eye. Blessed art thou, O Lord, who givest light to the whole world in thy glory. (Singer *Prayerbook*, page 438.)

The night prayer generally contains the sentences uttered by Jacob on his death-bed (Gen. 48:16, 49:18): "The angel who hath redeemed me from all evil, bless the lads . . . for Thy salvation I hope O Lord, I wait O Lord for Thy salvation." It closes with the hymn, *Adon Olom*, whose concluding sentence indicates that this hymn may originally have been a night prayer (cf. Chapter xv):

Into his hand I commend my spirit, when I sleep and when I wake;
And with my spirit, my body also; the Lord is with me, and I will not fear.

Tradition, referring to the phrase in Ezekiel (11:6), calls the Synagogue itself "the smaller sanctuary"; that is to say, that in reference to the great Temple on Mount Zion the various synagogues throughout the world were smaller sanctuaries, but it was these smaller sanctuaries which kept alive the spirit of devotion and maintained Judaism long after the Temple had lost its influence. It may well be said that the home is a smaller sanctuary in reference to the Synagogue, and it helped maintain the spirit of devotion in the individual family which, when brought into the Synagogue, gave the Synagogue much of its power and permanent influence.

XIX

I Will Praise His Word

COMMENTARY ON A SERVICE

THE Jewish prayer-service follows a characteristic range of ideas. While the services for the various holidays express certain specific thoughts which are not found in other services, nevertheless, the same essential moods and attitudes are found in all. While the various rites for different countries and of different centuries, likewise, vary from each other, the main spirit and direction is identical. The Prayerbook, for all its complications and variations, is of one texture; and as almost any section of a great painting can reveal the skill and the genius of the artist, so any prayer-service, closely studied, can reveal the ideals and the thoughts and the principles of the historic Jewish prayer ritual.

In this chapter we shall consider one service of the *Union Prayerbook* and present a running commentary to reveal its general Jewish mood and spirit, its variations, and its consonances with the rest of Jewish liturgy. The service to be studied is the Sabbath Morning Service in the *Union Prayerbook*, pp. 100 to 155.

Choir: *"How goodly are thy tents."* This opening paragraph is found in all rituals of northern Europe since the age of printing. It expresses the appropriate mood on entering the house of God: "I come to Thy house. . . . I bow down, and adore Thee . . . may my prayer be . . . acceptable . . . answer me according to Thy faithfulness." From the literary point of view the prayer is a typical evidence of how completely Jewish liturgy is influenced by the Bible. The whole prayer is a combination of verses selected from various parts of Scripture. The first verse: "How goodly, etc.," is from Numbers (24:5). It is the blessing of Balaam, the heathen prophet who was asked by Balak to curse Israel. He came to curse but remained to bless. The Talmud (b. Sanhedrin 105b) says, "The words 'thy tents' refer to the synagogues of Israel." This, of course, makes the sentence all the more appropriate for recitation on entering the synagogue.

The next sentence: "Through Thy great mercy," is from Psalm 5:8. The third sentence, "Lord I love, etc.," is from Psalm 26:8. The next verse, "And so I bow down, etc.," is from Psalm 95:6, but in order to fit with the grammatical form of the rest of the verses it is re-written from the plural as it appears in the Psalm to the singular. The last verse, "May my prayer be offered," is taken from Psalm 69:14.

The whole paragraph, therefore, is a collection of verses from various parts of the Bible expressing the joy and the privilege of coming into God's house. This type of prayer is typical of prayerbook-literature, a mosaic of appropriate biblical verses gathered from all parts of the Bible to express a specific idea.

The *Union Prayerbook* provides that this prayer be sung by the choir. This is in accordance with the established custom of the *Union Prayerbook*, namely, that every service begin in this manner, so that the attention of the worshipers be captured at once, and the service begin in a unified fashion.

On page 101, the prayer: *"The soul which Thou, O God, hast given unto me"*; is one of the regular morning prayers in all prayerbooks and is mentioned in the Talmud (b. B'rochos 60a) as a prayer to be recited on arising. All the early morning prayers were originally recited at home. In the Orthodox Prayerbook these early morning prayers came to be printed in the Prayerbook and have gradually grown and accumulated material from various sources. The *Union Prayerbook* selects a number of prayers from all this varied material, among them the prayer which we are discussing, "The soul which Thou, O God, hast given unto me came pure from Thee." The prayer is the staunch assertion of the Jewish belief that the soul does not enter the world with an hereditary taint of original sin, but, coming from God, is pure. The second prayer on the same page, "Lord of all worlds," also a regular part of the early Morning Service, is mentioned in the Talmud (b. Yomo 87b) as part of the atonement confession.

On page 102, "May it be Thy will," is a paraphrase of a number of similar prayers in the early morning prayers beginning with *"Y'hi rotson."* Most of these prayers are found in the Talmud Tractate B'rochos and are there given in the singular number, for they were the private prayers composed by certain rabbis to express their own moods and petitions. In the Orthodox Prayerbook, as here in the *Union Prayerbook*, this prayer is pluralized so as to be more suitable for public worship. The prayer as given here is not an exact translation but a paraphrase. A number of synonyms found in the Hebrew are omitted. As an example of the general style of simplification and paraphrase of older prayer material adopted in the *Union Prayerbook*, it would be interesting here to give the exact translation of the original text and the paraphrase in the *Union*

Prayerbook with it. The first two verses of the original (Singer *Prayerbook*, page 7) are as follows:

> And may it be thy will, O Lord our God and God of our fathers, to make us familiar with thy Law, and to make us cleave to thy command-ments. O lead us not into the power of sin, or of transgression or iniquity, or of temptation, or of scorn: let not the evil inclination have sway over us: keep us far from a bad man and a bad com-panion: make us cleave to the good inclination and to good works: subdue our inclination so that it may submit itself unto thee; . . .

The simplified paraphrase in the *Union Prayer-book* (page 102) is as follows:

> May it be Thy will, O Lord our God, to lead us in Thy ways, that Thy name may be honored and Israel be blessed by our actions. May we walk according to the precepts of Thy law, and, remaining firm in our devotion to Thee, may we never fall into temptation or shame.

"Early will I seek Thee" (page 103), a hymn, by Solomon Ibn Gabirol, written as a morning prayer, is found in many prayerbooks at the beginning of the service. The morning prayer material in the traditional prayerbook is so abun-dant that the *Union Prayerbook*, instead of using all of it at every service, has used part of it in one service and part of it in another and thus achieved a helpful variety from week to week. It will be noticed that pages 100, 103, 106, 111,

114, constitute five different openings for the five Sabbath Services that may occur in one month. The material in these openings is either from the morning blessings or from the morning Psalm-section (neither of which were originally part of the public Morning Service in ancient times). Thus, page 103 is the beginning for the second Sabbath of the month. The poem of Solomon Ibn Gabirol, discussed above (Chapter XVII), is a suitable beginning for the service since it speaks of prayer and the mood with which we approach God.

The prayer on the bottom of page 103, "With spirits uplifted," is an original prayer in the spirit of the liturgy asking for God's guidance that our prayer be worthy of utterance to Him.

The responsive reading, "Rejoice in the Lord," is a series of selected verses from Psalm 33; one of the regular Sabbath morning psalms (Singer *Prayerbook*, page 30). The psalms originally were recited responsively by the Levites in the Temple and also by the people in their worship outside of the Temple. The responsive readings in the *Union Prayerbook* are composed chiefly of psalm verses.

"Every living soul" (page 105) is a traditional prayer added to the Sabbath Service in the section of psalms. Originally, it seems to have been used for Passover and is still found in the Seder

Service. There was a curious legend current in France and Germany during the Middle Ages that this particular prayer was written by the Apostle Peter.

The introduction for the third Sabbath begins on page 106 with the famous Sabbath psalm, Psalm 92, "It is a good thing, etc." On page 108 is another original prayer, preparing the mood of the worshiper for prayer. The responsive reading which follows is not from Psalms but from Job and Isaiah. The *Union Prayerbook* continues the traditional literary habit of the Prayerbook of collecting verses from various sources in the Bible to create one unified prayer. (See above, page 270, discussion of "How goodly are Thy tents.") In this responsive reading the first verse, "Happy is the man," is from Job (5:17); and the answering verse from Job (5:18). The next verse, the sacrifices, is from Psalm 51:19; the next, "Unto God," is from Job (5:8, 9). The rest of the section is from Isaiah (40:27-31). The prayer that follows, "Thine everlasting arms," is, likewise, an original introductory prayer. It is interesting to note how in typical Prayerbook style the prayer is based upon biblical texts although it was recently written for the *Union Prayerbook*. The first sentence, "Thine everlasting arms, etc.," is taken from Deuteronomy (33:27). The third sentence,

"Darkness does not conceal Thee," is based upon Psalm 139:11, 12. In the fifth sentence, "The arrows of ill fortune that fly by day nor the pestilence that stalks by night," is from Psalm 91:5, 6 ff.

The final paragraph of this introductory portion for the Sabbath is the Twenty-third Psalm. It is strange that this famous psalm is so little used in the traditional Jewish Prayerbook. It is recited only on Friday night towards the close of the service in the ritual of the Chasidic Jews (*Nusach Ari*).

The choir hymn introducing the service for the fourth Sabbath of the month, is from the "Song of Glory," which was written in the thirteenth century and is traditionally recited on the Sabbath. On page 112 is the usual introductory prayer to create the mood of worship. The responsive reading that follows is taken from various psalms. The two first lines are from Psalm 119:1, 2; the next couplet from Psalm 119:89, 92. The next couplet is from Psalm 119:105, 118. The next couplet is from Psalm 19:13, 14. The next couplet is from Isaiah (32:17) and Psalm 119:165. The final introductory prayer, "Thou art One and Thy name is One," is a paraphrase of the prayer in the T'filo of Sabbath afternoon. (See the discussion of this prayer in Chapter XVI, p. 225.) In the history of the liturgy it was not unusual for prayers to be taken from their original place and used over again because of their especial effectiveness. Thus in the daily morning prayer the famous prayer, "Lord of all worlds," comes from the Atonement Service. The prayer, Nishmas, used for Sabbath at the end of the section of Psalms (P'sukei d'zimro) comes from the Passover Service. The great Adoration prayer, Olenu, was taken from the New Year Service where it introduces the sounding of the Shofor, but because of its universalistic mood it was finally placed at the end of every service. Certain prayers became favorites of the people and were used not only in their original place but also in another section to serve, as it were, "double duty."

In the introductory service for the fifth Sabbath of the month (page 114), the opening psalm for the choir is Psalm 122. This is one of the psalms used during the summer months for Sabbath afternoon. The next prayer on page 115, "Praised be He," is one of the introductory prayers to the Chapters of Song (P'sukei d'zimro) in the daily and Sabbath Services. The responsive reading which follows (Ashrei) is a traditional psalm combination in the Prayerbook. It begins with Psalm 84:5, then Psalm 144:15, then Psalm 145. This psalm sequence was greatly beloved by the early leaders of the synagogue;

indeed, the Talmud (b. B'rochos 4b) recommends that it be recited three times daily and so it is used in the traditional service. It is recited once in the Chapters of Song in the Morning Service, once after the T'filo of the Morning Service, and once before the T'filo of the Afternoon Service.

After these five introductions which use material from the early morning prayers and the Chapters of Song of the traditional Prayerbook, there follows the main part of the public service, the Sh'ma and its blessings. (Page 119 to the middle of p. 124, i.e., from "Praise ye the Lord," to "Praised be Thou our Redeemer, the Holy One of Israel.") The first blessing after the introductory formulae, "Praise ye the Lord," and the response is the prayer of God in nature, God the Creator. This prayer is the older and essential part of the prayer as found in the traditional Prayerbook. Certain hymns and descriptions of the various angels are omitted. The second prayer is the traditional prayer of God in history Who taught Israel the Law. The translation is somewhat paraphrased, repetitions and certain redundancies omitted. The original text (Singer *Prayerbook*, page 191) is as follows:

With abounding love hast Thou loved us, O Lord our God, with great and exceeding pity hast Thou pitied us. O our Father, our King, for

our fathers' sake, who trusted in Thee, and whom
Thou didst teach the statutes of life, be also
gracious unto us and teach us. O our Father, merciful Father, ever-compassionate, have mercy
upon us: O put it into our hearts to understand
and to discern, to mark, learn and teach, to heed,
to do and to fulfil in love all the words of instruction in Thy Law. Enlighten our eyes in
Thy Law, and let our hearts cleave to Thy commandments, and unite our hearts to love and fear
Thy name. . . .

The paraphrase simplifying the diction reads as
follows (*Union Prayerbook*, page 118):

Great has been Thy love for us and Thy compassion boundless. Our fathers put their trust in
Thee and Thou didst teach them the law of life.
Be gracious also unto us that we may understand
and fulfil the teachings of Thy word. Enlighten
our eyes in Thy Law that we may cling unto
Thy commandments. Unite our hearts to love
and revere Thee. . . .

Then follows the Sh'ma Yisroel on page 120,
and at the bottom of the page with the responsive reading, "True and enduring," begins the
blessing after the Sh'ma, called "The Redemption," because it deals with the redemption from
Egypt as evidence and promise of God's redemption of Israel from persecution. The text
of the closing part of this blessing is somewhat
universalized in the *Union Prayerbook* as follows (page 124):

· 279 ·

O Rock of Israel, redeem those who are oppressed and deliver those who are persecuted. Praised be Thou, our Redeemer, the Holy One of Israel.

Then follows the Sabbath T'filo (middle of page 124 to bottom of page 141) in accordance with tradition composed of seven blessings: the three introductory blessings, the intervening special blessing dealing with the mood and the sanctification of the day, and the three concluding blessings. The T'filo is marked for reading by the reader. The traditional Prayerbook has the T'filo of the morning as well as of the afternoon recited silently by the worshiper and then repeated aloud by the reader. But the ancient custom was to have the reader read it alone and the congregation merely respond, "Amen," (see Elbogen, *Der Juedische Gottesdienst*, page 28).

In the first of the three introductory blessings (page 124), there is a change of wording expressing a change in theological viewpoint. The traditional prayer towards the close of this prayer reads, "Who bringeth a redeemer to their children's children." The *Union Prayerbook* reads, "Who bringeth redemption." This is in accordance with the general principle of Reform congregations who do not hold to the old doctrine of a personal Messiah, a descendant of the House of David, but instead believe in a messianic age which is the essence of the traditional belief; hence, instead of a redeemer, the Prayerbook reads, "Redemption."

In the second blessing of the T'filo there is another change. The traditional prayer ends with the seal, "Praised be Thou Who revivest the dead." The *Union Prayerbook* ends, "Praised be Thou Who hast implanted within us immortal life." This difference in wording again represents a difference in theological point of view. The traditional Prayerbook believes in the resurrection of the body from the grave and its restoration to its former form. Reform Judaism believes in the immortality of the soul and not the resurrection of the physical body. The third blessing on page 126 containing the K'dusho (see Chapter XVI) is somewhat simplified from the form in the traditional Prayerbook. It omits as it did in the first blessing before the Sh'ma some vivid descriptions of the praise and flight of the angels, as Singer *Prayerbook*, page 190:

> Then with a noise of great rushing, mighty and strong, upraising themselves towards the seraphim, they exclaim over against them: "Blessed"

The paragraph beginning "One is our God; he is our Father," is taken from the K'dusho of the Sabbath Additional Service, Singer *Prayerbook*, page 228.

The fourth and intervening specifically Sabbath blessing begins on page 128. Just as the *Union Prayerbook* varies the introduction for the different Sabbaths of the months, so it varies the special Sabbath part of the T'filo—on page 128 for the first Sabbath of the month, on page 129 for the second Sabbath of the month, and so on for special Sabbaths, as the Sabbath during Sukos, Chanuko. This blessing, in its various forms, always ends with the traditional closing paragraph on page 138, "Our God and God of our fathers," with its seal, "Praised be Thou O Lord, Who sanctifiest the Sabbath."

Then follow the three concluding blessings of the T'filo, "Look with favor" (middle of page 138), "We gratefully acknowledge." In the traditional Prayerbook this second prayer of the three concluding prayers is given in two forms, one for the reader to recite and the other in a form somewhat different for the congregation to whisper while the reader recites his prayer. In place of these two simultaneous recitations of different texts, the reader and the congregation here read together the same text, "We gratefully acknowledge, etc."

On page 140, the third of the three concluding blessings, "Grant us peace," is somewhat paraphrased from the text in the Standard Prayerbook and as usual by the omission of redundancies which are not burdensome in the older Hebrew style but are unpleasing in English. Thus, Singer *Prayerbook*, p. 235:

Grant peace, welfare, blessing, grace, lovingkindness and mercy unto us and unto all Israel, thy people. Bless us, O our Father, even all of us together, with the light of thy countenance; for by the light of thy countenance thou hast given us, O Lord our God, the Law of life, lovingkindness and righteousness, blessing, mercy, life and peace; and may it be good in thy sight to bless thy people Israel at all times and in every hour with thy peace.

The simplified version in the *Union Prayerbook* (page 140) is as follows:

Grant us peace, Thy most precious gift, O Thou eternal source of peace, and enable Israel to be its messenger unto the peoples of the earth. Bless our country that it may ever be a stronghold of peace, and its advocate in the council of nations. May contentment reign within its borders, health and happiness within its homes. Strengthen the bonds of friendship and fellowship among all the inhabitants of our land. Plant virtue in every soul, and may the love of Thy name hallow every home and every heart. Praised be Thou, O Lord, Giver of peace.

Then follows the prayer of private devotion which closes the T'filo.

Originally this was not considered part of the T'filo proper but is one of the numerous private devotions of individual rabbis given in the talmudic tractate B'rochos to be recited after the T'filo. This particular prayer recited by Mar, son of Rabina (b. B'rochos 17a) became embodied in the T'filo. Some of the rest are scattered through the Prayerbook.

On pp. 142-143 is the half-hallel. The Hallel Psalms (the "full hallel," Psalms 113 to 118) are recited in the synagogue on festivals. The full hallel, the complete text of these Psalms, is recited on the main holidays (except the last six days of Passover); the half-hallel, that is, some of the Psalms omitted, is recited on the half-holidays, new moon, etc. On pp. 144-147 is the ritual for the reading of the Torah (see above Chapter IX). On page 147 the prayer, announcing the new moon, which is always recited on the Sabbath before the new moon, varies somewhat from the text in the traditional Prayerbook. The prayer at the bottom of page 147 and on page 148 is a combination of the various welfare prayers which appear in the traditional Prayerbook at this point in the service. Some of the prayers are from the g'onic period (i.e., the first post-talmudic period), Singer *Prayerbook*, page 219, middle of the page: "He who giveth salvation, etc.," to the bottom of page 220. These prayers, dating from various epochs, some g'onic, others medieval, and the last one for the welfare of the ruling dynasty still later, are combined here in this one prayer (pp. 148-149. "The Returning of the Torah").

At this point the traditional service for the Sabbath has another T'filo, the Musof or Additional T'filo, which corresponds to the additional sacrifice offered in the Temple on Mount Zion on Sabbath and holidays. Since this T'filo is largely sacrificial, it is omitted from the Reform Prayerbook.

On page 150, to the middle of page 151, there is the Olenu, or Adoration (see Chapter xiv). This prayer, likewise, is somewhat paraphrased from the form in the traditional Prayerbook. The universalistic hope of this great prayer is retained and emphasized but certain phrases omitted, such as: "He hath not made us like the nations of other lands, and hath not placed us like other families of the earth." The traditional text: "When Thou wilt remove the abominations from the earth and the idols will be utterly cut off, when the world will be perfected under the kingdom of the Almighty, and all children of flesh will call upon Thy name, etc.," is rewritten as follows: "We fervently pray that the day may come when all men shall invoke Thy name, when corruption and evil shall give way to purity and goodness, when superstition shall no longer enslave the mind, nor idolatry blind the eye, when all who dwell on earth shall know that to Thee alone every knee must bend and every tongue give homage."

On page 151: "And now ere we part" is the beginning of the prayer before the Kaddish. In the traditional Prayerbook the Kaddish, the great prayer of praise to God (here pp. 152-153) is found in many forms and is used frequently during the service. In the Reform Prayerbook it is given one standard form and is used only at the end of the service. It is provided with introductory prayers in English (see also the various introductory prayers to the Kaddish in the Friday Evening Service, pp. 72-75). The text of the Kaddish itself has one paragraph not found in the traditional Prayerbook, the paragraph beginning, "*Al Yisroel*" and the corresponding English paragraph, "The departed whom we now remember." This paragraph begins like one of the paragraphs in the traditional Kaddish of the Rabbis, but its text specifically refers to the departed.

The closing hymn, page 154, *Ein Kelohenu*, is discussed in Chapter xv. The English version, "Who is like Thee," is not a translation of the Hebrew but is a poem on the same theme by James K. Gutheim.

This study of a service in the *Union Prayerbook* indicates the differences characteristic of the Reform ritual: the abbreviation of certain texts which have accumulated through the centuries such as the early morning prayers, the omission of the Musof, the rewriting of certain prayers omitting redundancies, and the oriental modes of expression. But basically the service represents the same fundamental structure and content, the same literary style based upon biblical sources and in the new prayers the same creativeness under older inspiration, revealed at every stage in the development of the Jewish Prayerbook.

XX

Times and Seasons

THE CALENDAR

THE Jewish service cannot be understood without some knowledge of the Jewish calendar. The dates of the festivals, the observances of the festivals and even the daily services are affected by the nature of the calendar system. The following brief description of the calendar contains most of the data needed for an understanding of the services.

A. The Day. The Jewish day begins at sunset and ends at sunset. This is indicated in the statement in Genesis which says, "And there was evening and there was morning one day" (Gen. 1:4), "and there was evening and there was morning a second day" (Gen. 1:8). The evening is mentioned first as the beginning of the day. In Leviticus (23:32) the observance of the Day of Atonement is described as "from even unto even." While the day begins at sunset, nevertheless, in order that every worshiper may know exactly when the evening actually starts, the rule is that the evening begins at the moment when three stars can be seen in the sky. Thus every Sabbath begins on Friday evening; Passover, which is on the fifteenth of *Nison*, begins on the evening at the close of the fourteenth; Shovuos, which is on the sixth of *Sivon*, begins on the evening of the fifth. The forty-nine days (the *Omer* days) from the second day of Passover to Shovuos (Pentecost—i.e., the fiftieth day) is counted first on the evening ending the first day of Pesach and then every evening until Shovuos. The Evening Service at the end of the day of the festival no longer belongs to the festival but is the first service of the next day. Hence, in the Prayerbook Service for the Sabbath, the Friday Night Service is a Sabbath Service, the Saturday Night Service is a Week-day Service. The service for the night of the ninth of *Tishri* is the Kol Nidrei Service of the Day of Atonement; the Evening or Ma-ariv Service of the tenth of *Tishri* is an ordinary Week-day Service.

The days of the week have no individual names as in the western calendar except the Sabbath day which is so named. Of the other days, Sunday is known as the first day, Monday the second day, etc. Friday is known as Erev Shabos, the day before the Sabbath, while Monday and Thursday are special days. In ancient times they were the market days. People gathered from the farm lands into the cities. They were also days when the courts convened. Hence, the custom of reading the Torah in the Morning Service on those days arose. The reading consists of the first section of the weekly portion for the coming Sabbath. Likewise, penitential prayers (Singer *Prayerbook*, page 70 ff.) are recited. Pious people fast on certain Mondays and Thursdays during the year.

B. The Week. The idea of grouping the days into sevens, in other words, of dividing time into weeks, was not known in the Roman Empire until it was introduced by Jews and later by Christians. The origin of the week seems to have been Babylonian, perhaps derived from the four phases of the moon, the new moon, the first quarter, the full moon, and the third quarter, which are roughly seven days apart. Originally, the seventh day was considered an unlucky day but Judaism converted it into a holyday of rest (see Chapter xi). Although the days have no name, except Friday and Saturday, in the Jewish calendar the weeks have names derived from the portion of the Torah read that week. Thus, the Sabbath of Genesis, the Sabbath of Noah, the Sabbath "Go Thou" on which the story of Abraham's mission is read, the Sabbath "And He appeared," on which the story of God appearing to Abraham is told, the Sabbath "Life of Sarah," etc.

Certain Sabbaths are named after the prophetic portions, rather than after the Torah portions, such as the Sabbath of Comfort when the fortieth chapter of Isaiah is read beginning with the words, "Comfort ye, comfort ye, My people"; or the Sabbath of Vision, when the first chapter of Isaiah is read (the Vision of Isaiah the son of Amoz). Other Sabbaths have special names owing to special readings or observances; thus the Great Sabbath, the Sabbath before Passover, or the Sabbath before Purim which is called the Sabbath of "Remember" because of the special reading, "Remember Amalek" (Exod. 17: 8-16). The week begins with Sunday and ends with the Sabbath.

C. The Month. The Hebrew month is lunar as were the months in all ancient calendars. The month is the period from new moon to new moon. The period from new moon to new moon, that is to say, the time that it takes the moon to go around the earth, is approximately 29½ days. Since a month obviously cannot begin in the middle of a day, therefore, the lunar month is either 29 days or 30 days, depending on whether the half-day is reckoned with the preceding or with the following month. In ancient times the sages determined the length of the month (i.e., whether it should have 29 or 30 days, that is, whether the new moon should begin on a certain day or on the following day) by requiring people who saw the new moon to come before the court, the Sanhedrin, and testify that they saw it. The court would question them closely to discover whether they really saw the moon or some other light which may have deceived them. When the court was satisfied that the witnesses had really seen the new moon, it proclaimed that day to be the new moon and the beginning of the next month. Then the court would order signal fires lighted on the mountain-tops to announce to the people the rise of the new moon. Thus the people knew when the month began and could observe the festivals on the correct day.

Those people who lived far away from Palestine and who could not, of course, see the signals, would be uncertain as to when the new month began. Hence, they could not observe the festivals on the exact day required by the biblical law. For example, Passover was to last for seven days beginning with the fifteenth of *Nison*. But those who lived outside of Palestine and did not see the bonfires lighted by the order of the court when the new moon was proclaimed, could not know whether the preceding month had 29 or 30 days. Since they were in doubt about only one day (because if the preceding month had 29 days, the next month would have 30 days), they made sure that they celebrated the festivals correctly by adding one day to the festivals. Thus, outside of Palestine, Passover, which biblically is seven days, became an eight-day festival; Shovuos, which biblically is a one-day festival, became a two-day festival, etc. By the third century of the present era lighting bonfires and sending messengers to announce the date of the new moon had ceased and the calendar was based mathematically upon astronomical calculations. Now all Jews wherever they lived could know the exact length of the month. Nevertheless, they did not revert to the biblical observance of seven days for Passover and one day for Shovuos. In modern times, however, Reform congregations readopted the biblical length of the festivals which, of course, had persisted in Palestine all through the centuries.

It seems that originally the months were not referred to by separate names but were called "the first month," "second month," etc. Thus, in Leviticus 23, the festivals are dated by numbered months. However, the Bible does retain traces of ancient names, the name *Oviv* (Springtime) (Exod. 13:4); *Ziv*, the second month (1 Kings 6:1); *Esonim*, the seventh month (1 Kings

8:2); and *Bul*, the eighth month (1 Kings 6:38). After the Exile the Babylonian names of the months were used, namely, *Nison, Iyor, Sivon, Tamuz, Ov, Elul, Tishri, Cheshvon, Kislev, Tebet, Sh'vot, Ador*. These names are still used in the Jewish calendar.

The beginning of each month was an important holiday in biblical times. Special offerings were prescribed for the Temple on that day (Num. 28:11-15). The prophets frequently refer to the day as a holiday. Jewish liturgy today has a special New Moon Service with a special T'filo and reading of part of the Hallel Psalms. On the Sabbath before the new moon, the coming new moon is announced (Singer *Prayerbook*, page 219; *Union Prayerbook*, page 147). Originally the Shofor was blown at the beginning of every new moon (Num. 10:10) but in later times the blowing of the Shofor was restricted to the new moon of the month of *Tishri*, i.e., the New Year.

D. The Year. Twelve months of 29½ days amount to a year of 354 days, which is approximately 11½ days less than the sun year. Thus after three years of twelve lunar months the moon year would be 33 days (or more than a month) behind the sun year. If, for example, Passover, which must be celebrated in the spring, were celebrated according to the twelve-month lunar calendar, it would after three years be celebrated in the winter. The moon year, therefore, needed to be corrected so as to correspond with the sun year, upon which the seasons depend. It was this need for keeping religious festivals at the right season which led to the correction of the lunar calendar among all peoples.

The moon calendar can be moved to catch up with the sun calendar in various ways. Eleven days could be added at the end of each year, or after three years a full month could be added. In early days a practical method was used to determine whether it was necessary to add an extra month that particular year. The people knew that the barley harvest, which was the earliest of the grains to ripen, was usually ripe by Passover. The officials would go out to the fields and judge the state of the crops. If they saw that it was impossible for the barley to be ripe by Passover, they knew that the calendar was sufficiently behind the sun year, to require the addition of an extra month. Therefore, the next new moon was declared not that of the month of *Nison* but of the Second *Ador*. Nowadays the leap year is determined by a mathematical system. In a group of nineteen years the leap-month, the Second *Ador*, is added seven times. When there is a leap year, the festival of Purim is celebrated in the Second *Ador*.

As to which month of the twelve is the first month of the year, the Mishnah (Rosh Ha-shono 1, 1) says that there are four new years as we would say: a calendar year, a school year, a fiscal year for the government, etc. The first of *Nison* is described as the new year for kings; kings' reigns were counted from the first of *Nison*, that is to say, if a king ascended a throne six months before the first of *Nison*, when the first of *Nison* came it was the beginning of his second year. The first of *Tishri* is called the "new year for years"; that, as far as the Jewish Prayerbook is concerned, is the religious year. Thus the new moon of the month of *Tishri* is the New Year. The chief festivals as they appear in order in the calendar are:

TISHRI FIRST	*New Year*
TISHRI TENTH	*Day of Atonement*
TISHRI FIFTEENTH	*Sukos*
KISLEV TWENTY-FIFTH	*Chanuko*
ADOR FOURTEENTH	*Purim*
(2ND ADOR IN LEAP YEARS, THE 14TH)	*Purim*
NISON FIFTEENTH	*Passover*
SIVON SIXTEENTH	*Shovuos*

There are exactly forty-nine days or seven weeks from the second day of Passover to Shovuos, the Feast of Weeks. Therefore, Shovuos always occurs one day later in the week than the first day of Passover. There are ten days, counting both ends of the group of days, between New Year and the Day of Atonement. Therefore, the Day of Atonement always comes two days later in the week than the New Year. Since there is also a rule that the New Year can never occur on Sunday, Wednesday, or Friday, the Day of Atonement, which is two days later in the following week, cannot occur on Tuesday, Friday, or Sunday.

E. The Era. The Bible (Lev. 25) speaks of the groups of seven sabbatical cycles of seven years which were to be combined into one jubilee period. According to the Mishnah (Sanhedrin v, 1) witnesses testifying to a certain event were asked, "In what sabbatical period of the Jubilee, in what year, on what day did the event occur?" Evidently they reckoned the years by jubilees. This system was not widely practiced. The Bible does not date events by jubilees, but according to the year of each king's reign.

In the time of the Maccabees and since then until about the twelfth century the Jews used the era of Seleucus, the successor of Alexander in western Asia. This era of Seleucus was used in dating documents and became known in Jewish literature as the year of Deeds. The era now in use became prevalent about the twelfth century and refers back, traditionally, to the creation of the world.

Bibliography

DAVIDSON, ISRAEL, *Thesaurus of Medieval Hebrew Poetry*, Vols. I-IV, Jewish Theological Seminary, New York, 1924-1933.

DAVIS, NINA, *Songs of Exile*, Jewish Publication Society, Philadelphia, 1901.

ELBOGEN, ISMAR, *Der Juedische Gottesdienst*, G. Fock, Leipzig, 1913.

FREEHOF, SOLOMON B., *The Book of Psalms, A Commentary*, Union of American Hebrew Congregations, Cincinnati, 1938.

HASTINGS, JAMES, *Encyclopedia of Religion and Ethics*, 12 Vols., Scribners, New York, 1908-22.

Jewish Classics Series, Jewish Publication Society, Philadelphia.

Jewish Encyclopedia, Funk and Wagnalls, New York, 1901.

KOHLER, KAUFMANN, Jewish Theology, Macmillan, New York, 1929.

——, *The Origins of Synagogue and Church*, Macmillan, New York, 1929.

SALAMAN, NINA, *Selected Poems of Jehudah Halevi*, Jewish Publication Society, Philadelphia, 1924.

SCHECHTER, SOLOMON, *Some Aspects of Rabbinic Theology*, Macmillan, New York, 1923.

SCHECHTER, SOLOMON, *Studies in Judaism*, Jewish Publication Society, Philadelphia, Series I, 1896; Series II, 1908; Series III, 1924.

Service of the Synagogue, George Routledge & Sons, Ltd., London, 1904-20.

SINGER, SIMEON and ISRAEL ABRAHAMS, *Companion to the Daily Prayerbook*, Cambridge University Press, London, 1922.

Standard Book of Jewish Verse, compiled by Joseph Friedlander. Dodd, Mead & Co., New York, 1917.

ZANGWILL, ISRAEL, *Selected Religious Poems of Solomon Ibn Gabirol*, Jewish Publication Society, Philadelphia, 1923.

Index

Adon Olom, 55, 114, 204 ff.
Adonoy, 198 f.
Adoration, 183 ff.
Afternoon Service, its origin, 43 ff., 119
  for Day of Atonement, 175
  for the festivals, 154
  for the Sabbath, 133
Amida, 75
Avodo, 39

Babylonian Exile, 27 ff.
Bible, 16
  and New Year, 163
  ritual for Day of Atonement, 171 f.
Birchos Hashachar; *see* Morning Blessings

Cabalistic movement, 92
  influence on Sabbath Eve Service, 128
Chanuko, 265
Chasan B'reshis, 155
Chasan Torah, 155
Chol hamo-ed, 151
Christianity, dependent upon Synagogue, 24
  of Scriptures, 100 f.
Confirmation Ritual, 158

Day, 288 ff.
  begins at sunset, 288
Day of Atonement, 162 ff.
  biblical ritual, 171 f.

Ein Kelohenu, 196 ff.
Elohim, 198 f.

Era, 297
Esrog, 148
Ethics of the Fathers, 140
Evening Service, 120
  for Day of Atonement, 173
  for New Year, 164
  its origin, 43 ff.
Ezra, 30 f., 34

Festivals, names and dates of, 296 f.
Friday Evening Service, 127

Gabirol, Solomon Ibn, 204, 230 ff., 250
Gaon Amram, 197
G'ulo (Redemption), 68, 253

Halevi, Jehuda, 230 ff., 252 ff.
Halevi, Solomon al kabetz, 128, 212 ff.
Half-Kaddish, 190
Havdolo, 134, 262 f.

Isaac, Simon ben, 244

Jannai, 241
Jose ben Jose, 241
Josephus, 96

Kabolas Shabos (Sabbath Eve Service), 127
Kaddish, 188 ff.
Kalir, Eleazar, 241
Kalonymus, Meshulam ben, 244
Kalonymus, Moses ben, 244
K'dushas Hayom, 260

· 300 ·

Kiddush, 131, 262
Kol Nidrei, 173, 192 ff.

L'cho Dodi, 128, 212 ff.
Lulov, 148
Luria, Isaac, 265

Ma-a-modos, 41, 50, 176
Ma-ariv, 42; *see also* Evening
    Service
Mincho, 42; *see also* After-
    noon Service
Mohammed, 25
Monotheism, 19 f.
Month, 291 ff.
    names of, 293 f.
Mooz Tsur, 265
Morning Blessings, 112
Morning Service, 48
    for Day of Atonement, 174
    for New Year, 166
Musof, 43
    for Sabbath Morning, 133

New Year, 162 ff.
    product of Synagogue and
        Prayerbook, 163
N'ilo, 45, 176
Nishmas, 225

Olenu, 183 ff.
Omer, 147 f.
Omnom Ken, 248 f.
Ov (Ninth Day of), 105

Passover, 144
    home service, 263 f.
    Temple ritual, 146
Pharisaic movement, 40 f.
Pharisees, 34 f.
Pilgrim Festivals (R'golim),
    145
Piyut, 239 ff.
    beginnings in Palestine, 241
    in Morning Service for
        New Year, 244 ff.

Piyut—(*Continued*)
    use of acrostic, rhyme and
        meter, 239 f.
Prayerbook, 10
    changed to fit the needs of
        Israel, 15
    communion with God, 21
    contains religious ideals, 16
    influence on human history,
        12
    influence on Jewish life, 13
    petitional prayers, 74
    reference to redemption
        from Egypt, 69
    spiritual worship, 24
Prayerbook of Gaon Amram,
    197
Prayers, Personal, 89 f.
    for the New Year, 93 f.
Priestly Blessing, 178 ff.
Prophets, public reading of,
    97
Psalms, 33
    almost entire bulk of ser-
        vice, 52
    earliest prayers, 54
    greatest biblical influence
        on the Prayerbook, 49
    lyrical poetry, 51
    set style of Prayerbook, 55
Psalms (Hallel), 50
Psalms (Hallelujah), 57
Psalms (Sabbath), 57
P'sukei d'zimro (Chapters of
    Song), 73

Rav, 185
Redemption from Egypt, 69
Redemption Poems, 253 f.

Sabbath, 123 ff.
    as described in the Bible, 125
    as found in the Prayerbook,
        126
    home ritual, 259 f.
    spiritual mood of, 137 ff.

Sabbath Afternoon Service, 133
Sabbath Morning Service, 131 ff.
Sabbath Service, 122 ff., 126 ff.
Safed, 214 f.
Saturday Evening Service, 134
Scriptures, 99 ff.
   annual cycle reading, 99
   influence on Christian church, 100 f.
   public reading of, 95 ff.
Sermon, 100
Services for Holidays, 151 ff.
Shacharis, 42; see also Morning Service
Shikchi Y'gonech, 251
Sh'ma Yisroel, 59 ff.
   essential part of Evening Service, 120
   for New Year, 166
   for Sabbath Eve, 137
   for Sabbath Morning, 131
Sh'mini Atseres, 151
Sh'mone Esre, 74 f.
Shofor Ritual, 166 f.
Shovuos, 144
   relationship to Confirmation, 157 f.
Simchas Torah, 151, 155
Song of Unity, 228 f.
Sukos, 144
   Temple ritual, 146 f.
Synagogue, 10
   influence on Christianity, 13
Synagogues, their origin, 36 ff.

Talmud, 11 f., 16
   legislation for observing the Sabbath, 128 f.

Temple, 36
   sacrificial service, 43
T'filas Tal, 148
T'filo, 40, 75 ff.
   concluding blessings, 86
   corresponds to regular offerings of the Temple, 76
   essential element of Afternoon Service, 119
   for Evening Service of Day of Atonement, 173
   for Morning Service of Day of Atonement, 174
   for New Year, 164, 166
   for Sabbath Afternoon, 133
   for Sabbath Eve, 130 f.
   for Sabbath Morning, 131 f.
   Jewish ideal of prayer, 86 f.
   part of Evening Service, 120
   petitional prayers, 77 ff.
   praises of God, 81 ff.
   three main divisions, 76
Tomid, 43

Un'sane Tokef, 229

Week, 290 f.
   special names of, 290 f.

Year, 294 ff.
   festivals of, 296 f.
Yetser Ha-tov, 115
Yetser Ho-ro, 115
Yigdal, 55, 209 ff.
Yizkor (Memorial Prayer), 154
Yomim Noro-im, 162
Yotser, 59 ff.

Z'miros, 265